AUTHENTIC SHADOW WORK WORKBOOK & JOURNAL FOR BEGINNERS

Unlock Your Shadow Self, Increase Emotional Intelligence And Start Healing Your Wounded Inner Child & Subconscious Trauma

10 EXTRA MATERIALS INCLUDED INSIDE

LAUREN. J. ABRAHAM

CONTENTS

	PAGE
CONTENT	2
1. Introduction to Shadow Work	3
- What Is a Shadow?	4
- The Jungian Perspective	6
- Why Is Shadow Work So Important?	7
- Setting the Stage for Shadow Work	8
2. Grow and Heal with Shadow Work	10
- The Transformative Power of Shadow Work	11
- The Challenges That You Might Face	12
- Joining Your Shadow to Your Aware Self	14
- Navigating the Journey	15
3. Unearthing Wisdom through Self-Reflection	19
- The Importance of Self-Reflection	20
- Getting to Know Your Real Self	21
- Inner Child Work	22
- **Activity 1:** Guided Questions for Self-Exploration	27
4. Self-Compassion and Self-Care Meditation	31
- Visualization	35
- **Activity 2:** Guided Visualization Meditation	37
- Inner Dialogue	38
- Art Therapy	39
5. Dream Analysis: Deciphering the Language of the Unconscious	42
- The Process of Dream Analysis	43
- Benefits of Dream Analysis	44
- **Activity 3:** Dream Recall and Record	46
6. The Power of Positivity: Harnessing Affirmations in Shadow Work	47
- Affirmations: More Than Just Positive Thoughts	48
- Mastering the Art of Positive Affirmations	49
- **Activity 4:** Beginner-Friendly Affirmations	51

	PAGE
7. Navigating Through Emotional Waves	55
- Types of Discomfort That Come with Shadow Work	54
- Strategies for Handling Emotional Discomfort	55
- Dealing with Fear of Facing Painful Emotions	57
- **Activity 5:** Fear Flow Exercise	60
- When to Get Professional Help	61
8. Dealing with Shadow Work Reactions	63
- Recognizing Your Triggers	64
- **Activity 6:** Three, Two, One	66
- Unveiling	67
- Hidden Patterns	67
- **Activity 7:** Three Steps to Recognize Your Self-Sabotaging Patterns	69
9. The Power of Shadow Work Journaling	71
- Why Journaling Works	72
- Getting Started with Shadow Work Journaling	75
- Tips and Techniques for Using a Shadow Journal	78
- Emotional Journaling Techniques	80
- **Activity 8:** Journal Prompts for Emotional Journaling	82
10. The Mystery of Archetypes: Unveiling Invisible Forces	91
- The Essence of Archetypes	92
- Archetypes and Complexes	95
- Navigating the Archetypal Landscape	97
- **Activity 9:** Self-Archetype Quiz	99
11. The Long-Lasting Rewards of Shadow Work	102
- Mental Well-Being	103
- Embracing the Lifelong Journey	105
- Finding Your Shadow Work Community	106
- Expanding Your Shadow Work Knowledge	107
- **Activity 10:** The Mirror	109
CONCLUSION	110

1. INTRODUCTION TO SHADOW WORK

The concept of the shadow refers to aspects of our personality that the conscious mind is unaware of or doesn't recognize within itself. It encompasses the entirety of the unconscious, representing the parts of ourselves that remain unknown or hidden in darkness. In simpler terms, the shadow can be understood as the hidden or unacknowledged side of our being.

The shadow, being an instinctive and irrational aspect of our psyche, tends to attribute to others the flaws that we unconsciously perceive within ourselves. It is human nature to avoid blaming ourselves, which leads us to conceal these aspects of our personality, attributing them to others rather than acknowledging them as a part of us. However, by disregarding or denying this side of ourselves, we inadvertently grant it the authority to manifest the very things we despise or fear the most.

Eliminating your shadow would be akin to dividing yourself in half. Both elements are necessary for equilibrium and completeness. Instead, our aim is to illuminate those hidden areas so that you can perceive them with clarity rather than remaining oblivious. Eventually, you will reconcile with these challenges and harness them for your benefit. However, this transformation will not occur instantaneously; rather, it will resemble the gradual peeling of layers from a colossal onion.

When we mention our hidden side or the part of ourselves that we keep hidden from others, we are talking about the emotions such as anger, fear, sadness, rejection, shame, denial, and embarrassment that we all suppress deep within ourselves. The reason behind this behavior is that since childhood, we have been taught that these emotions are not acceptable. As a result, we navigate through life wearing a fake mask and burying these emotions further into our inner selves.

What Is a Shadow?

When you hear the word "shadow," you may think of something bad or harmful, which may lead you to see shadow work as a spooky and sinister task that makes us confront our undesirable traits. But we're not just good, we have a dark side, too. And this is why our shadow seems dark. But it's part of us and we needn't worry about accepting all parts of ourselves.

Carl Jung, a Swiss psychologist, was the first to bring the idea of the shadow to Western culture. In Jung's view, the shadow is the hidden pieces of our personality that our active mind overlooks or keeps hidden. It holds the parts of us that are out of our sight (*The Psychology of the Unconscious*, 1912).

We were born as whole individuals, but lose this wholeness as we grow. Our shadow side takes shape in our youth due to our interactions with those closest to us. The folks who take care of us shape our beliefs about which parts of ourselves are okay and which are not. The pieces labeled as "bad" are dismissed and these become the shadow side of us.

Shadow work helps us look at our hidden self, or "shadow self." This part of our mind holds thoughts and feelings we don't often think about. They might be things that we're embarrassed or upset about. These suppressed thoughts are sometimes called "shadows." They may be hidden away because they make us feel bad or remind us of difficult times.

To improve self-awareness, shadow work guides us to face these hidden parts of us, our "shadow side." By embracing our darker parts, we can find the brighter parts within us. Carl Jung used four archetypes to describe personality traits. One of these was the "shadow." This shadow represents the parts of us that we keep hidden. These hidden parts might seem negative, but Jung thought that they were an essential part of who we are (*Psychological Types*, 1921).

The shadow could be doubts, anger, negative beliefs, or deep emotional scars. It includes all the hard parts of life and can be tough to explore. Shadow work helps us explore these hidden thoughts and feelings. It aims to improve our self-understanding, strengthen our relationships, learn more about our minds, and heal from past wounds.

Throughout our lives, people give us feedback about who we are. They make judgments based on how we behave and react to things. We take in all this feedback. But only keep the parts that fit with how we like to see ourselves. We throw away feedback that doesn't fit. In this way, we try to build up a picture of ourselves that reflects who we want to be.

But, there's more to us than the self we show others and the self we believe ourselves to be. Everyone has a shadow. When it stays hidden from our conscious mind, it grows bigger and darker.

Those parts of us that we're not aware of can get very complex. You could picture it like a dark room in a house that never gets any light. We have to shine the light of awareness on these dark corners within ourselves.

Our actions are influenced by our subconscious and unconscious minds, often referred to as our shadow self, as suggested by certain professionals. These aspects of our mind hold deeply ingrained belief systems and thoughts, which we may not be consciously aware of. Typically, these beliefs and thoughts originate from our childhood experiences. Consequently, it is not unexpected that these concealed facets of our personality play a significant role in behaviors that undermine our own success.

In our quest to manifest our desires, many of us tend to overlook the unconscious factors that influence our daily behavior. Instead, we tend to concentrate on what is already apparent to us. These hidden aspects, including our repressed desires and unacknowledged parts, are referred to as "the shadow." Discovering and addressing these internal workings is crucial in achieving our goals.

Many of us are unaware of the contents within our shadow, and these neglected aspects might still be influencing the way our reality is shaped.

Our subconscious or the shadow self, operates without conscious awareness of whether it is working against us or not. Due to its hidden nature, it can subtly influence our lives, beliefs, and behavior in unforeseen ways. In some cases, it may even manifest as protective mechanisms meant to shield us from displaying our true power and vulnerability to others. Consequently, it becomes imperative to bring the shadow self to light and engage in inner work to establish a meaningful dialogue between ourselves and our "dark side" in order to facilitate positive transformation.

The Jungian Perspective

In the realm of Carl Jung's theory of analytical psychology, shadow work holds immense significance. It provides a deep understanding of the human mind and involves exploring and finding harmony with our hidden, suppressed, or rejected personality traits, known as the "shadow self." Jung believes that embracing and unlocking the potential of our shadow self is crucial for achieving psychological wholeness and personal growth.

According to Jung, the shadow self represents the parts of us that we don't usually acknowledge or fully connect with. It includes both negative traits, like anger, envy, and greed, as well as positive traits that we may have overlooked, such as creativity and assertiveness. The shadow self is made up of the unconscious aspects of our being that we've pushed down deep inside ourselves. Our thoughts, behaviors, and emotions are heavily influenced by our unconscious mind. Hidden within this unconscious realm is the shadow self, which holds suppressed and unrecognized thoughts and feelings. This concealed content can profoundly impact various aspects of our lives, often surfacing indirectly and shaping the choices we make and the relationships we build. So, it's important to acknowledge and understand this hidden side to better navigate our lives.

When it comes to personal growth, Jung believed that embracing our shadow self is crucial in becoming our true and genuine selves. He called this process "individuation," which is an ongoing journey toward embodying our most authentic and complete version. By integrating the shadow, we learn to recognize and reconcile the different aspects of our personality, leading to a more balanced and harmonious self. It's like embarking on a lifelong adventure to discover and unite with our true essence.

According to Jung, symbolism and dreams are closely connected, and the shadow often emerges in our subconscious minds. By studying these symbols and images, we can gain valuable insights into the essence of the shadow. Dreams, in particular, provide a wealth of psychological content that can be explored through psychoanalysis.

Why Is Shadow Work So Important

Embracing your shadow self is a key part of personal growth and development. Here's why it's important to understand and accept this side of yourself.

Why not let your shadow self take the driver's seat sometimes? It could be beneficial to see things from a new angle.

JUNG'S IDEA

Jung said that accepting our shadow self is the key to psychological completeness. By acknowledging and integrating this part of us, we develop a deep understanding of ourselves. This process removes hidden insecurities, leading to a sense of self-confidence.

BETTER RELATIONSHIPS

Our shadow self can impact our relationships through things like defense mechanisms. For example, sometimes we place our own hidden feelings onto others, causing misunderstandings. Accepting our shadow self helps us own our feelings and actions, leading to healthier relationships.

ELIMINATING CONFUSION AND NEGATIVITY

Expressing our shadow self can be confusing. It can lead to new behaviors and emotions that we don't understand. This happens because we've just hidden these feelings, not gotten rid of them. If we're angry but don't express it, that anger will come out later in a twisted way, often directed at someone innocent. It's like holding a ball underwater eventually, it's going to pop up. The effort to keep it under strains us, leading to more problems like anxiety or depression. By accepting and integrating our shadow self, we learn to manage these feelings, which lessens negative behaviors and feelings.

IMPROVE UNDERSTANDING AND SELF-LOVE

It's important to know all parts of ourselves, even the less than great bits. When we understand and accept these parts, it can really let our talents and creative ideas flow. Things like meditation, creating art, journaling, and expressing our shadows visually can help them come out into the light. This leads us to know ourselves better and feel more connected. Always remember that when you're doing these activities, ask your inner critic to be open and curious, not critical. With this mindset, your inner critic will feel more comfortable stepping out and opening up.

GROWING THROUGH SELF-ACKNOWLEDGMENT

Having our shadow side as part of our lives is key for personal growth. When we recognize and address our shadows, we can start to like and respect all parts of ourselves. This process of learning about ourselves leads to a deeper level of self-understanding and self-love. So, accepting our shadow side can be a big help for personal growth and self-improvement.

Embracing the shadow in us allows us to reach a healthier mental state, strengthen our bonds with people around us, lessen the power of bad feelings, build empathy, and further our development as individuals.

Setting The Stage For Shadow Work

Shadow work is important and setting up the right space helps a lot. You need a quiet, cozy place. It could be in your house, outside, or another private space. It's got to feel safe. Have things like a journal or craft supplies nearby to jot down your feelings. Before you start, know what you're aiming to do. It helps keep your thoughts on the right track. Set a schedule for your shadow work. It can be every day, every week, or just now and then. But keep to it! Use mindful strategies or grounding sessions to keep you anchored in the "now." If feelings get tough, have someone around to support you. Self-care routines and being kind and adaptable to yourself are key. This environment will help your shadow work. It paves the way for a deep, emotional journey and personal growth.

Here's how you can set the stage for shadow work:

PICK YOUR SPOT
Find a simple, quiet place. It can be a room, an outside area, or a private spot that makes you feel safe and cozy.

NO DISTRACTIONS
Keep the place free of distractions. Make sure to switch off gadgets and adjust the lighting to keep it soft. The key here is to allow for deep thinking.

COZY AREA
Choose comfy chairs or pillows. A relaxed place can help you to open up emotionally.

HAVE TOOLS READY
Keep items handy, like a diary, pens, or craft supplies, which help in expressing yourself. They can help in penning down thoughts and feelings.

OUTLINE YOUR GOALS
Fix clear goals before you begin your self-discovery. What do you want to heal or learn? Setting goals helps your sessions to stay focused.

MINDFULNESS
Use mindfulness techniques to stay grounded. Deep breaths, meditation, or body scans can aid with relaxing your mind and being in the moment. This helps in exploring emotions.

EMOTIONAL SUPPORT
Make sure you have emotional backup. It can be a friend, therapist, or helpline. Emotional support can assist in dealing with tough feelings.

SELF-CARE RITUALS
Integrate self-care rituals into your space. These could include soothing elements like candles, soft music, or calming scents that promote relaxation and emotional well-being.

FLEXIBILITY AND SELF-COMPASSION
Embrace flexibility and self-compassion in your practice. Allow yourself the space to adapt as needed, acknowledging that some days may be more emotionally challenging than others.

CLOSURE AND INTERGRATION
After each session, take time for reflection and integration. Journaling about your experiences, insights gained, or emotions felt during the session aids in processing and integrating the work done.

Getting ready for shadow work also needs a deep change in thinking. You must be ready for a brave, deep dive into learning about yourself. Part of the prep is being open and ready to face uncharted parts of one's mind. Acknowledge the deep feelings you may confront. Realize that shadow work means digging into your subconscious to discover hidden parts of you. By recognizing this, you'll be primed to tackle your mind's hidden corners, even if they're uncomfortable.

This journey requires boldness. You must face old wounds, triggers, and parts of you that have been put aside. You must be ready to meet fears, doubts, and buried feelings. Why? Because understanding them is key to healing and self-improvement. Building up this spirit is an important part of psychologically preparing for shadow work. While the journey may be tough, the inner findings and healing can greatly change you for the better.

Also, learning to be kind to yourself is crucial. Understand that the trip through shadow work can cause feelings of vulnerability, self-doubt, or emotional turmoil. Being self-compassionate means being forgiving and kind toward yourself. Accept that vulnerability comes with being human, that these hard emotions are valid and need to be faced for healing. Cultivating a tender inner conversation helps make a safe emotional environment where you can explore yourself without self-blame or criticism.

Believe in yourself and in the shadow work process because it's a vital part of getting ready mentally. To believe in yourself is to trust in your resilience and inner strength. It means being sure that you can handle the emotions and memories that show up during the process. You need to believe that you can face and include these parts of you. This can help you understand and accept yourself more fully.

Next up, be patient. Healing and finding yourself through shadow work doesn't happen right away. It's a constant, changing process. Being patient means knowing that this journey has its ups and downs. It's about being kind to yourself and letting things happen in their own time. Knowing that every step, no matter the size, moves you forward on your healing journey.

In short, getting ready mentally for shadow work means having an open mindset, bravery, self-love, trust, and patience. It's a starting phase that sets you up for a transformative inner journey. This journey will lead you toward self-discovery, healing, and a deeper self-acceptance and completeness.

2. GROW AND HEAL
WITH SHADOW WORK

Exploring your shadow self can lead to personal growth and healing. Your shadow self is a mix of things about you that are often hidden and might make you uncomfortable. Comprehending that you're not just the good part of you, but also some darker sides, is essential in this journey.

Working with your shadow self can raise self-awareness. This means looking closely at hidden parts of you. As you come to understand these areas, you'll learn more about who you are. This learning lets you make choices that truly reflect what you want and value. It's like looking in a mirror that shows every part of you, even the complex ones.

Doing this work often leads to emotional healing. Your shadow self might have emotions, past traumas, and fears locked away. Working though these emotions can start your healing. It might feel like examining old hurts, cleaning them, and then fully healing them. Completing this process feels like a huge burden has been lifted. This can allow you to move on with emotional clarity and strength.

Working with your shadow self can spark personal growth. Your shadow self isn't just a place for bad traits, it's a goldmine of unused talents and strengths too. By recognizing and embracing your shadow, you get to use these hidden talents. Think of it as finding secret treasures within you. These treasures can make your life better in many ways.

Besides personal growth, shadow work can improve relationships. As you learn more about your own reactions, biases and assumptions, you can better understand others. This leads to real, peaceful relationships. You're less likely to shift your unresolved issues onto others. So, you become a better listener, speaker, and supporter, leading to healthier, more satisfying relationships.

The Transformative Power Of Shadow Work

The effective changes triggered by shadow work are deep and complex. They dig into our subconscious, exposing hidden aspects of ourselves. This process begins a powerful change within. It provides a road to impressive self-development, emotional recovery, and self-understanding.

In simple terms, shadow work is a key to emotional freedom. It involves facing hidden feelings, unsolved upsets, and unknown parts of our minds. We begin a path to find out more about ourselves and to heal. By digging deeper, we let these hidden emotions come up, recognize them, and give ourselves the okay to understand and let go of them. This emotional freedom helps to make us stronger. It builds a strong base for us to grow more in the future.

Yet, the change shadow work brings goes beyond just letting out emotions. It reaches past simply recognizing these unseen parts and tries to add them into our conscious mind. When we accept and include overlooked pieces of ourselves, a deep feeling of completeness appears. The broken self starts to come together, and self-approval flourishes. This including is a way of self-kindness and comprehension, lessening the burden of self-criticism and forming an inside place where all sides of our being receive recognition and peace.

Shadow work reveals key insights about ourselves. Like a flashlight in the dark, it shows us unseen parts of our mind. With this new understanding, we can make sense of our habits, shaped by hidden aspects of ourselves. Breaking free from these hard-set behaviors, we can better face life's challenges. This gives us control and helps us understand why we act the way we do.

Exploring our shadows can shift our relationships. As we get to understand ourselves more, we start observing our thoughts and hidden prejudices. It all leads to realness, kindness, and stronger bonds, which are the heart of our connections with others. These bonds are built without biases and offer deep connections, making room for real love and understanding.

In addition, acknowledging our shadow sides can boost creativity and originality. It wakes up abilities and talents we didn't realize we had. Parts of our persona that we were not aware of can now be used in creative ways to solve problems. As a result, we come up with one-of-a-kind ideas, art projects, and lifechanging solutions.

Ultimately, the main strength of shadow work is that it helps us become whole, tough, and genuine. It is a deep process of understanding ourselves better, gaining confidence, and healing that goes beyond just recognizing the shadow. We gain a clear outlook of ourselves as we accept and work with our shadow, and it leads to a happier and more meaningful life.

The Challenges That You Might Face

Shadow work may transform and enlighten, but it's surely no easy stroll. View it as facing your own hidden depths, your buried sides that have stayed under wraps for a long time. It's akin to lighting up your mind's neglected corners. While this can be uplifting, it also could prove demanding. Let's peek at some possible obstacles during shadow work:

DEALING WITH RESISTANCE

See resistance like your own defense to change. Imagine its function—to keep things as they are. The mind builds a fortress to hide aspects of yourself you could find uncomfortable. It's a survival tactic, pushing against change feels like stepping into unknown territory. Being in a comfort zone feels secure, leaving it can spike feelings ofconcern and fear. It's okay to feel scared when you start questioning the actions you've upheld, value systems, or personal stories you've created. This can be tough, but it initiates growth. It's okay to feel off balance, or even afraid, right on the verge of a new phase.

EMOTIONAL UPS AND DOWNS

Diving into your hidden aspects can stir up strong emotions. You may find yourself grappling with anger, sadness, fear, and shame. Usually, these emotions are hidden away because they can tip the balance, making it hard to stay steady. You might feel like you're on a whirlwind emotional ride from time to time. However, this emotional storm is an expected part of exploring your hidden aspects. Picture it as a snow globe shaken up, things might look messy but will eventually settle, giving a clear view. It's crucial during this emotional exploration to have support, maybe a friend, a therapist, or a journal to put down your thoughts.

DIGGING-UP PAST HURTS

When exploring your shadow, you could uncover old, painful memories. These are often hidden away deeply, because they're emotionally heavy. Looking at them again feels a bit like poking old bruises. It's thoroughgoing work and can feel like you're scratching at restful scars. Handling these memories gently is key. It's subtle work—you can take it slow. Getting professional support like therapy can be beneficial, providing both advice and a safe zone to look at these memories.

SELF-JUDGMENT

Shadow work involves facing the parts of you less flattering. It's easy to be hard on yourself when revealing your shadow. Feelings like guilt or shame might creep up, or feeling a bit disappointed in yourself. The deeper you go, the stronger these feelings might become. But, self-kindness is vital here. Instead of picking at yourself, try to deal with your shadow warmly and patiently. Remember that everyone has their flaws, and this ride is about understanding and growth, not self-blame. Self-kindness will cool these harsh thoughts and help you push on with a healthier perspective.

VULNERABILITY

Opening up to your shadow requires you to be vulnerable. It's not easy to admit that you have flaws, insecurities, and dark sides. This vulnerability can be uncomfortable because it means revealing your hidden aspects to the light. It can make you feel exposed, like you're standing in front of a mirror that reflects not just your best self, but all your imperfections too. However, vulnerability is not a weakness; it's a source of strength and growth. Through vulnerability, you can accept yourself more deeply and connect with others authentically. Embracing vulnerability is a courageous act that empowers you.

FACING YOUR FEARS

When it comes to shadow work, one important aspect is confronting your fears and anxieties directly. This can feel overwhelming because it requires stepping outside your comfort zone and challenging deeply rooted beliefs and behaviors. These fears might be linked to past traumas, insecurities, or the fear of change. The process can be like standing on the edge, uncertain of what lies beneath. However, facing your fears is essential for personal growth. Only by acknowledging and addressing these fears can you break free from their grasp and experience a newfound sense of freedom and self-confidence.

TIME AND PATIENCE

Shadow work takes time and patience. It's not a quick fix or an instant solution. Unraveling and integrating your shadow self can require months, or even years, to see significant progress. This can be frustrating because we often want immediate results in our efforts to improve ourselves. However, it's important to be patient with the process. Think of it like tending to a garden. You plant the seeds, nurture them, and wait for them to grow. Every small step you take is an important part of your personal growth journey. Embrace the gradual nature of this process and avoid unnecessary self-criticism and frustration.

FEELING ALONE

Doing shadow work can often seem like you're doing it by yourself. This is because others might not fully understand or back your journey inward. This might make you feel alone or cut off. Sometimes, people around you won't really get what you're up to. Or, they might feel uneasy talking about it. In such situations, finding a therapist, counselor, or a supportive group can help a lot. These can provide a safe place to talk about what you're going through, get advice, and feel heard. Making contact with others also doing shadow work can be very helpful. It will provide a sense of fellowship and confirmation.

Joining Your Shadow To Your Aware Self

After you've discovered your shadow, the next trick is to join it with your aware self. This can be tough because you need to strike a balance. You have to recognize your shadow aspects, but not let them control you. It's not good to suppress or deny them, but neither is it wise to let them dominate. It's like learning to dance with your shadow and knowing it's part of you. This balance requires self-understanding, kindnessto yourself, and regular thoughtfulness. Through practice, you can blend the different sides of you, bringing a more complete and truthful expression of yourself.

Many people have a difficult time with the feeling of not knowing what's about to happen next. It can arise when you're stressing over something that's coming up or when you feel like you have little to no control over a particular situation, or you're in an environment you aren't very familiar with. This fear tends to manifest itself in different ways different ways, like avoiding doing certain things, feeling physically uncomfortable, or going through mental turmoil.

Exploring the depths of our thoughts and beliefs through shadow work can feel like an uphill battle. It requires us to confront the unknown, burst out of our bubbles, and venture into uncharted territory. This journey of self-discovery can stir up many emotions, but it's crucial for our personal growth and development. By embracing this path, we have the chance to face our fears heads on, understand ourselves on a deeper level, and achieve success.

Don't worry too much at this time, go ahead and take that leap! You have all the capabilities to start the process of shadow work, and you'll be pleasantly surprised by the new perspectives you'll gain about yourself and the world. Let's tackle these challenges together and overcome them!

Remember, though, that shadow work requires that you show kindness toward yourself and that you embrace and acknowledge any fears that you have without being overly critical of yourself. This book will serve as your safe place and provide you with a supportive environment. Keep in mind that there's no one correct way to navigate through this process. Take your time and proceed at your own pace, without feeling pressured.

Initially, venturing beyond your familiar territory can feel quite daunting. We often prefer to stick with what we are familiar with and shy away from anything that causes even the slightest discomfort. However, over time, you will come to realize that remaining within your comfort zone prevents you from fully embracing the countless extraordinary experiences that life has to offer.

You could start by taking small steps and trying out new experiences, like exploring unfamiliar places or engaging in conversations with familiar faces. With each step taken outside of your comfort zone, you will gradually build up confidence and develop a greater sense of readiness to tackle more significant challenges. So go ahead, take those risks and watch yourself grow!

Navigating The Journey

When embarking on the exploration of your inner shadows, it becomes crucial to ensure your energy levels are high, you are grounded, and mentally prepared to confront the deeply buried issues from your past. Incorporating a practice of meditation can serve as an excellent starting point for both initiating your journey and identifying these shadows. It is important to note, however, that this path is not an easy one, and some of the challenges you encounter may evoke emotional distress. Thus, it is advisable to be mentally and emotionally prepared for the transformative work that lies ahead.

Below are some tips to get you started:

START SLOWLY

Engaging in shadow work can be mentally and physically draining. Individuals embark on a deep introspective process that resurfaces forgotten memories, which have been repressed over time. It is advisable to start slowly, focusing on one shadow at a time. Beginning with meditation can help identify the shadows that manifest during these reflective sessions. Once a shadow has been chosen, it is essential to journal extensively. This allows for the identification of the qualities and aspects of the shadows that have an impact on one's life, as well as how they relate to these aspects.

Elusive shadows tend to hide themselves deliberately, requiring the use of defense mechanisms to keep them at bay. To fully address these shadows, we must exercise patience and devote a good amount of time. Being frustrated is perfectly normal during this stage. Find comfort in relaxation techniques such as deep breathing exercises. There are no time constraints or deadlines for you to complete your shadow work journey. You have full autonomy to work at your own pace without any expectations.

You must recognize that the process of illuminating your unconscious mind requires significant effort and regular practice. It is not a one-time task, but rather an ongoing endeavor. The more attention you devote to your emotions and behaviors, the greater your ability to discern the hidden aspects of yourself and fully comprehend them.

PAY ATTENTION

In order to identify shadows within ourselves, it can be useful to observe how we react to others. Pay close attention to your responses during moments of stress, anxiety, or irritation, for example. By doing this, you can pinpoint the triggers that directly relate to these shadows. It's important to recognize that these triggers have been conditioned within you. They are the aspects you have suppressed and tried to overlook for a long time, yet they still impact you emotionally and may occasionally show themselves in form of erratic behavior. By acknowledging this, you can gain a deeper understanding of the effects caused by your shadows.

It is important to acknowledge that anything that stresses or agitates us may actually be a part of ourselves that we have disowned. This realization can be an enlightening moment in recognizing our own shadows. It is at this point that the real work begins, as it paves the way to embrace and support the entirety of our persona.

Now, the focus shifts to self-identification. During the process of shadow work, it is essential to acknowledge and understand your own emotions and their origins in real time. Engaging in shadow work may lead to various triggers that were previously overlooked, coming up as new obstacles. However, as you persist in this journey, you will gradually understand the emotions you project outwardly (ego, conscious behavior) and those you conceal internally, as your body language and reactions inadvertently expose your subconscious responses (the shadow effect).

In the realm of human existence, it is important to remember that each individual possesses their own unique set of inner struggles. These personal struggles, although varying in nature, are shared among the collective human experience. However, not everyone openly displays their emotions on a consistent basis. Within every person, there lies a diverse range of qualities, both positive and negative, awaiting the catalyst that will bring them to the surface. The shadow work process involves self-reflection and comprehension of one's own emotions and triggers, as well as the ability to observe and identify what causes certain reactions in others.

SELF-TALK AND INTUITION

As you delve into the realm of shadow work, a noticeable shift will occur in your internal dialogue. Internal dialogue refers to the self-talk that occurs inside of your mind, providing commentary on your surroundings. It serves as the avenue for the application of personal knowledge and understanding in various situations. However, it is important to recognize that this voice is uniquely your own.

During the process of shadow work, intuition may also come into play, lending its guidance. It presents itself as a voice that is acknowledged but distinct from our internal dialogue. It is very important to understand that this experience is natural and does not signify a loss of sanity. Rather, it marks one of the most important milestones in the journey of shadow work.

When we disregard our internal dialogue, we are basically neglecting our ability to confront our inner struggles. Such a choice can be perilous as it allows the shadow to exert its influence more freely on our emotions and actions. Neglecting self-talk often leads to self-sabotage, which can become a recurring issue in personal growth and development.

Conversations with ourselves play a vital role in gaining understanding. Engaging in dialogue with the shadows within allows for the spread of love, kindness, and compassion to the darkest corners of our mind. Rather than being perceived as unknown adversaries, our shadows become acknowledged aspects of our being that aid in personal growth and enlightenment. Embracing these shadow elements gradually leads to a sense of wholeness that we might not have felt before.

WHOLENESS AND UNDERSTANDING

As you go through these steps, you will gradually develop an understanding of your shadow traits and how they came to be. It is really important to integrate the characteristics of these shadows into your conscious self, so that you are able to identify them when they emerge in your real life experiences. Essentially, you need to incorporate these qualities into your being. It's important to remember that these traits don't define who you are; rather, they contribute to your overall wholeness as they already exist within you.

By incorporating these shadow traits within yourself, you rectify the mistakes made by suppressing and denying them in the past. These qualities have not vanished but rather remain buried within your mind. You must pay attention to your projections and triggers, and merge them into your personal understanding of your actions and the construction of your identity. Accepting these qualities may bring discomfort as they might not align with your current perception of self. But, remember that your ego will resist this process. It is up to you to fight the urge to not acknowledge your negative habits.

Through the process of shadow work, we are able to assimilate the fragmented aspects of our personality into our conscious mind, ultimately achieving a sense of wholeness. This introspective journey provides a much more profound understanding of ourselves, leading to a much greater sense of inner peace. By embracing love, kindness, compassion, and understanding within the darkest parts of ourselves, we form a genuine understanding of who we truly are at the core.

SELF-AWARENESS

The primary objective of engaging in shadow work is to attain self-awareness, a profound understanding of one's entire being. This transformative journey requires ample time and patience. You must progress at a speed that suits you, sustaining ease in the undertaking. By accepting and making peace with your unearthed aspects, you lay down the road to inner calm and balance.

Every person has a sunny side they recognize and root for. Yet, often tucked out of sight, are pieces of us made of feelings or hard times we're afraid to unveil. Exposing hidden parts of ourselves is a challenge shadow work presents us. This exploration enables us to make important self-discoveries. As we keep digging, we come across significant insights that promote healing and boost personal development. It's quite a journey!

BONUS PAGES

By purchasing this book, you gain access to exclusive bonus content designed to complement your journey through the "Authentic Shadow Work Workbook & Journal For Beginners." This special gift includes guided meditations, visualizations, daily affirmations, and more, all crafted to deepen your understanding and enhance your practice of shadow work. To access your free content, simply scan the QR code at the bottom of this page with your smartphone's camera, and follow the link that appears.

QR

Enjoy this thoughtful addition to your self-discovery journey!

3.
UNEARTHING WISDOM THROUGH SELF-REFLECTION

Self-reflection, a part of shadow work, is of extreme significance. Like a flashlight, it lights up secret corners of our selves. It helps us see parts we weren't aware of. Think of it like a self-odyssey or a "You" journey.

We do self-reflection to look inside us. We stop to ponder, ignoring distractions around. We focus inward to our inner world. In this special time, our hidden parts come forward. Honesty and open mindedness guide us into our psyche's depths.

During self-reflection, we also get a chance to view our thoughts and emotions neutrally. We just observe without any judgment. We see how we think, feel, and behave. We watch the bonus beats of our inner world. This helps us understand our subconscious better. We see how it affects our life.

As we shine the inner light, secret memories come out. Emotions we forgot pop up suddenly. Bits of our personality that we pushed away or forgot show up. Going through this can be tough sometimes. It means dealing with our fears and insecurities. However, this gives a chance for real healing and growth.

The Importance Of Self-Reflection

Self-reflection also allows us to identify and examine the patterns and behaviors that no longer serve us. We gain insight into the underlying causes of our self-sabotaging tendencies or limiting beliefs. By bringing these patterns to our conscious awareness, we empower ourselves to make conscious choices and create positive change in our lives.

Moreover, the practice of self-reflection serves as a catalyst for developing a profound understanding of oneself. This self-awareness, when nurtured, becomes a valuable tool for personal growth. It grants us a clear vision of our core values, aspirations, and authentic identity.

As a result, our intuition becomes more attuned, empowering us to make choices that align with our highest potential. Through self-reflection, we acquire the ability to differentiate between our true essence and the external influences that have shaped us.

Incorporating self-reflection into our daily lives allows us to maintain an ongoing dialogue with ourselves. It becomes a regular practice of checking in, reassessing, and realigning. It provides us with the opportunity to celebrate our progress, acknowledge our achievements, and course correct when needed.

Shadow work also involves compassion and self-love. These are key in our path to change and rebuild. They help us meet our hidden fears with care and understanding, not judgment.

Shadow work walks us into spots within ourselves that have deeply hurt us. Here we encounter parts of ourselves which may be wounded or need healing. These shadows might reflect past hurts, emotional scars, or aspects of the self we view as bad. When we face these, compassion is an ally. It encourages us to treat ourselves with gentleness and understanding.

Compassion lets people accept, not avoid, their darker parts. It's a wise friend teaching them to forgive and be kind to themselves when diving deep into their self. This kindness builds up a safe and caring place where they can face, accept, and heal their shadows one step at a time.

Shadow work has self-love as its core. It's a deep recognition of our own value and our right to personal growth. Self-love lets us meet ourselves with love, patience, and total acceptance when exploring our inner shadows deep down.

When we start liking ourselves a lot, we begin to realize that our problems don't mark who we are. Our problems are not as a drawback, rather these are ways for us to become better and change. We start feeling better when we start taking better care of ourselves; confirming our efforts to making a good life for ourselves.

To really like ourselves, we need to be kind to ourselves, create healthy boundaries, and do things that are good for our body, heart, and spirit. This means we appreciate what makes us special and recognize even our small wins. Self-love nudges us to look after our own needs, accept our feelings, and build a caring bond with ourselves.

By creating this bond of self-love and compassion, we can make a deep bond with ourselves and also, with others. This method brings light to the fact that our common problems connect us, making us believe that we're not on our own. This understanding enables us to show empathy and kindness to others who are also trying to discover and improve themselves.

Getting To Know Your Real Self

Deep inside the work we do on ourselves, lies the attempt to be real. It uncovers the path of finding and accepting your real self, free from society's demands, mental conditioning, and self-made limitations. Encouraging authenticity in this work allows you to dig into and combine the parts of you that have been hidden or pushed down.

Shadow work is like a safe place, helping people get to know their real selves. It allows them to peel off the labels that society has put on them. They can question deep seated fears and beliefs that keep them from feeling like themselves. It's a process that helps them take back their personal strength, align with their deepest values, and live truthfully to chase their dreams.

When people do shadow work, they face parts of themselves they've ignored or denied. They might have been told those parts aren't good enough. It might be hard at first, but those "shadows" have important wisdom. They can help people grow. Accepting and understanding these shadows can lead to a deep awareness of their true selves.

Being authentic in shadow work means being open and brave. The person dives into their feelings, thoughts, and hopes without judging or hiding anything. This allows them to celebrate their unique experiences and viewpoints. As a result, they can shine their true selves without holding back.

When a person accepts who they truly are, big changes can happen. They find new confidence and freedom. The need to fit in with others or look for approval goes away. Instead, they're okay with embracing their own truth and expressing themselves, even if it scares them.

Shadow work is all about finding your true self. It's like peeling back layers, revealing what's behind the roles we play and expectations we have. It makes us question the stories that created us. The goal? To rewrite our own story, forming a strong and real self-image.

Inner Child Work

Shadow work and inner child healing go hand in hand. They help us navigate our emotions, affecting how we feel and act. Shadow work lights up hidden places where past hurts might be hiding. This hurt may come from unpleasant experiences as a kid, such as neglect or trauma. They stay with us deep down, affecting our thoughts, actions, and feelings.

Shadow work helps us find these hidden pains. It lets us face and work through pain we may have ignored. When we do this, we often run into parts of our "inner child." This is our younger self, still hurt by past experiences. Encountering these hurt parts of ourselves is a chance to reconnect. We can take care of and recognize our younger self that wants to heal.

The more that we do shadow work, the more we connect our current self with the secrets of our past. It's like building a bridge. We don't try to forget the past. Instead, we work to help the inner child heal and feel safe. This is a bit like becoming a parent to our own inner child. It means showing care, love, and kindness that we might have missed out on when we were younger. By showing compassion to our inner child while doing shadow work, we start to heal emotionally. It helps us to accept ourselves, be resilient, and find inner peace.

HEALING THE INNER CHILD THROUGH SHADOW WORK

Shadow work can help heal wounds left by your inner child. This process is made of self-reflection, thorough introspection, and kind care of your younger self. Shadow work is a powerful tool for helping our hurt inner child. With it, we can carefully and softly help the parts of us that are still carrying the pain from when we were young. This work dives deep into our minds and brings up the old hurt and feelings that come from our past. We often find that these old feelings tie us to our inner child and show us where we are still hurting.

Our path to feeling better starts when we bring this old hurt up to the surface. As we find and think about these hidden feelings, we make a safe place for our inner child to let go of old pain that's been hidden away. It means that we need to think hard and look closely at ourselves, with kindness. It's giving understanding and care to the hurt inner child in us.

Shadow work also gives our inner child the touch of kindness they need. As we do this work, we give love, care, and help to the young parts of us that didn't get enough when we were growing up. It's a little bit like being a parent to ourselves, hugging our hurt parts in a gentle way that helps us feel better about ourselves.

In all of this, putting everything together is very important. Instead of trying to forget or get rid of our old hurts, we accept them and bring them into our everyday lives. We let our hurt inner child become part of who we are, not something we hide. By helping and accepting our hurt inner child, shadow work lets us heal emotionally, accept ourselves, and be strong.

Shadow work, at its core, is a healing journey. It's like we're taking care of the younger and more delicate parts within us. This journey lets us understand our past better. It helps us be kinder to ourselves, be more aware of our feelings, and find internal peace. Healing our inside, our "inner child," through shadow work, is a big step. It helps us feel emotionally better, complete, and kinder to ourselves.

Here are easy steps to help you navigate this transformation.

LOOKING BACK AND REALIZING

Start with your past, specifically your childhood. Look for emotional habits, triggers, or old issues that may be from your early years. Knowing these habits starts your healing.

WRITING AND PERSONAL LOGGING

Make time for writing. Jot down memories from your childhood, emotions, and big events. Look deeper into these experiences and how they may have shaped you. Writing it down lets you express thoughts, fears, and doubts openly.

INNER CHIT-CHAT AND MIND PICTURES

Practice inner conversations or visualization. Picture your younger self and talk kindly to them. Console, reassure, and encourage your inner child. Imagine making a safe, loving space for them.

SEEING TRIGGERS AND FEELINGS

Be aware of triggers or strong emotional reactions in your life now. Look at these feelings and think about how they may connect to old wounds from childhood. This realization helps identify where to heal.

HANDLING FEELINGS AND LETTING GO

Let yourself experience and evaluate emotions from past events. Do things that aid in releasing these stifled emotions. For instance, write letters you won't send, use art as expression, or try mindfulness to understand and accept feelings openly.

SELF-CARE

As a way of nurturing your inner self, adopt self-soothing activities. Practice positive self-talk and form habits that foster security and calm.

PROFESSIONAL HELP

If necessary, seek advice from therapists versed in healing past wounds and shadow work. Their expertise can provide useful guidance and resources.

ACCEPT YOURSELF

Blend lessons learned from your introspective work into your daily life. By recognizing, and accepting your past you allow self-growth. Remember that healing is a journey, and each step matters.

ESTABLISH BOUNDARIES

Set sensible boundaries in life to safeguard against reliving painful experiences. Introduce self-care habits that take care of your thoughts, body, and spirit.

FORGIVENESS AND EMPATHY

Learn to forgive yourself and others who may have caused past pain. Be compassionate and understanding with your younger self throughout the healing journey.

Take note that working through inner child trauma is very personal. Be patient and kind with yourself as you tread this life-changing course of healing and self-understanding.

CHALLENGES WITH INNER CHILD HEALING

Healing your inner child's wounds isn't easy. It's like battling a storm of powerful emotions that spring from sad and scary experiences of the past. Sometimes, feelings like heavy sadness, fiery anger, or deep down fear can pop up. They may have been buried or unhandled for a long time. Facing these emotions can shake you up and scare you. But you need to be tough and aware to steer through these emotion storms.

Also, meeting your inner child's fragile side requires that you open up emotionally. It could be uneasy. It means going back to harsh or neglected times. This reunion may at first sharpen the hurt or feeling of being left alone. You need to make an emotionally secure space for your inner child. This has to be a safe space which might not have been there in your early years.

A further challenge is the dread or hesitation linked with looking at these deep seated wounds with adult eyes. At times, a hidden defensive shield could hinder digging deep into these hurtful memories or emotions. This unwillingness can come from a dread of reexperiencing the trauma, feeling bad or guilty about past events, or thinking the pain is too much to face. Overcoming this unwillingness and bringing a feeling of security within self is key to progressing with the healing work.

Healing hidden hurts from your past can seem scary. It means stepping back and looking at old stories and thoughts. It also means seeing how past stuff influenced how you act and think now. This makes some people feel weird or unsure, as they face parts of themselves forgotten or ignored.

Also, walking this healing path can feel lonely sometimes. People around you might not get why you're digging deep into emotional stuff. This can make you feel even lonelier, making the healing heavier.

Working through hard stuff takes patience and perseverance. Often, getting help from counselors, support groups, or understanding friends can be needed. These folks can guide, make you feel valued, and offer a good place for expressing feelings. Even with hard parts, healing your past can bring big positive changes. It can lead to being free of old emotional weight, knowing yourself better, and being kinder to yourself. It can make you tougher, too.

Healing inner child wounds can be tough. But don't worry, below are tips to make it easier:

BE KIND TO YOURSELF
Healing takes time. It's okay. Show yourself some love. Do things you enjoy. Meditate, relax, pick up hobbies.

FIND YOUR SAFE ZONE
Find a quiet, comfortable, distraction free place. This will help your inner healing.

ASK FOR HELP
Don't be afraid to get professional help. Therapists or counselors can provide great tools and a safe space to help you heal.

LEARN HOW TO COPE
Emotions can swell up. But techniques like deep breathing, grounding exercises, or journaling can help you stay calm.

STAY IN THE MOMENT
Be aware of your feelings and triggers. It can help you understand reactions due to inner child wounds. This is called mindfulness.

TAKE TINY STEPS
The healing journey is a marathon, not a sprint. Avoid overwhelming yourself. Take one step at a time, no rush.

WELCOME VULNERABILITY
Accept vulnerability as a tool for development. Permitting oneself to feel, recognizing vulnerability as an integral part of healing, is key.

ENGAGE WITH POSITIVE PEOPLE OR GROUPS
Look for supportive friends, groups, and communities where you feel both heard and affirmed. Discussing life experiences with those on a similar path can enhance your sense of belonging and validation.

ESTABLISH LIMITS AND ADVOCATE FOR YOURSELF
Draw clear lines to safeguard your emotional stability. When you need room, help, or self-care time, have the courage to speak up for what you need.

APPRECIATE PROGRESS
No matter how small, always celebrate your progress. Value the bravery and resilience required in this journey of healing.

Navigating the process of healing historical hurts requires bravery and leads to transformation. Patience with oneself, self-compassion, and reaching out for help, are crucial as you journey toward self-understanding and well-being.

ACTIVITY 1:
Guided Questions for Self-Exploration

These cues are a springboard for self-reflection and exploration while doing shadow work. They stir up a thorough thought process of the unseen parts of yourself. This leads to understanding yourself better, accepting yourself with kindness, and finally, finding a route toward combining all parts of our being and healing.

Ask yourself the following questions and write the answers.

1. Uncovering Shadow Aspects

What aspects of myself do I have the tendency to hide?

....
....
....

Are there any recurring patterns of behavior that I have difficulty accepting?

....
....
....

What sorts of insecurities do I try to avoid?

....
....
....

2. Exploring Emotions

Which emotions do I have a hard time expressing in my day-to-day life?

....
....

Do I have emotions that I find unacceptable?

....

....

....

What kinds of things trigger extreme emotional responses within me?

....

....

....

3. Examining Beliefs and Values

What beliefs or values do I hold that might come from social conditioning rather than my own true self?

....

....

....

Do I hone conflicting beliefs within me that cause an internal struggle?

....

....

....

How do these beliefs influence the decisions I make, and are there any that I'm reluctant to look at more closely?

....

....

....

4. Reflecting on Relationships

How do my relationships mirror parts of my hidden self?

Do I see any patterns? Are there ongoing issues in my relationships that could be connected to my own unresolved issues?

Do I attribute specific characteristics or feelings to others that I might be hesitant to recognize within me?

5. Exploring Childhood Experiences

What events from my childhood could have played a part in creating my shadow side?

Have I stashed away or find it hard to return to some of my past memories?

In what ways could these memories sway my current actions or feelings?

....
....
....

6. Self-Reflection and Integration

What methods can I use to better understand and accept my shadow sides?

....
....
....

How can I welcome and acknowledge these traits without feeling scared or biased?

....
....
....

How can I respect and gain insight from my shadow self to aid my self-improvement and recovery?

....
....
....

4.
SELF-COMPASSION AND SELF-CARE

Being kind to oneself and having patience are key when doing shadow work. They help people work through their feelings and inner discoveries with a gentle, understanding approach.

In shadow work, being kind to oneself means treating yourself as you would a good friend going through the same stuff. It's about recognizing the tough spots that we each have inside us. These spots might be painful or filled with embarrassing or bottled up feelings. Instead of being hard on oneself or judging harshly, being kind means talking to oneself in a comforting, reassuring way.

This softens the emotional journey. It helps people embrace and make sense of experiences without harsh self-blame. Being patient is also important in shadow work. This means knowing that healing doesn't happen all at once or in a straight line. It happens slowly, in bits and pieces, at its own speed.

Patience lets people value their emotional growth. It helps them understand that healing includes revisiting and making sense of complex feelings. Patience is about accepting that understanding some parts of oneself might take time, and that's okay. Being patient means living in the moment, without hurrying or pushing for answers. It involves being okay with the back and forth nature of emotions—letting them rise to the surface, be recognized, and gradually folded into one's understanding of oneself.

When you mix self-kindness with patience, it makes for a loving inner world. This helps during reflex thinking. Instead of looking for answers right away or pushing hard feelings aside, this lets people feel their full scope of emotions. They see that even small steps help them learn and grow.

Also, growing self-kindness and patience builds toughness. It gives people emotional power to face tough feelings during reflex thinking. It allows them to handle strong emotions or hard memories with personal power and a soft touch to their own selves.

There are various ways to help you look after yourself on your shadow work journey. These methods include meditation, visualization, and art therapy, to name a few. This chapter will look at the various ways that you can look after yourself while carrying out shadow work.

Meditation

Shadow work meditation is a thought-focused exercise. Its goal is to explore and understand the unnoticed parts of our mind. It uses meditation as a digging tool for the hidden emotions and experiences that are often unaddressed, alongside undiscovered behavior patterns. When someone does this kind of meditation, they're likely to start in a calm, cozy spot. They might sit or lay down, using their breathing patterns as a grounding anchor. As they relax, they intentionally probe their thoughts, feelings, and past experiences. They do this without passing judgment or getting too attached. Sometimes, they may visualize coming face to face with their "shadow self." Or they might let previously held back emotions bubble up naturally.

While going through these mental experiences, they adopt a curious and understanding stance. They're not supposed to get stuck or fixated on certain thoughts or emotions. Instead, they aim to warmly welcome whatever pops up from the subconscious. In doing so, shadow work meditation promotes self-insight, emotional intelligence, and a way to blend these shadow parts into the conscious mind. This can result in personal development and healing.

Meditation is key to doing effective shadow work for a few reasons:

EXPLORING WITHIN YOURSELF
Meditation lets you delve deep into your thoughts, feelings, and memories. It becomes a home base for self-exploration. You gain access to parts of your mind which are usually hidden.

BECOMING MORE AWARE
Meditation helps you become more aware of what you are experiencing right now. It lets you see your thoughts, emotions, and reactions without judgment.

MANAGING EMOTIONS
Working through your shadows can bring up strong emotions. Meditation gives you ways to watch and handle these emotions. It creates a calm sense of self, which helps when dealing with difficult feelings

MAKING SPACE FOR PROCESSING
Meditation gives you a safe, quiet space inside yourself. You can use this space to work through and understand complex feelings and memories that come up during shadow work.

UNDERSTANDING YOUR SUBCONSCIOUS
Through meditation, you get to dig deeper into your mind. This unearths hidden thoughts, beliefs, and behaviors. You'll then be able to pinpoint and understand why you do certain things, linked to your 'shadow self.'

SELF-REFLECTION BOOST
Meditation helps with self-reflection. It's a stepping stone to understanding motivations, fears, and wants. It also lets us look at our hidden problems, helping us learn more about ourselves.

HEALING
Meditation makes our mind calm. This lets us bring our buried issues into our conscious minds. Through meditation, we can realize and embrace these issues without feeling bad. This boosts our emotional well-being and growth.

In the end, meditation is key to shadow work. It's a thoughtful, orderly way to understand our minds. Our subconscious can be confusing, but meditation gives us the tools we need. We can understand ourselves better, manage how we feel, and work toward integrating our hidden issues.

Here are some meditation techniques to help with shadow work:

MINDFULNESS MEDITATION
Pay attention to your breath and body. This anchors your focus on the here and now. When thoughts or feelings appear, watch them without bias or clinging. This method helps you be more self-aware and lets you "see" shadow traits when they show up

GUIDED IMAGERY
Try meditations that are made just for shadow work. These lead you through pictures or stories that help you confront your shadow self safely.

INNER CHILD MEDITATION
Picture talking to your own inner child. Imagine you're interacting with yourself as a kid. This treat yourself nicely practice helps you explore and heal things from your past.

CHAKRA MEDITATION
Focus on certain energy spots (chakras) in the body. You visualize these areas and check for any blocked energy or feelings. This may help reveal shadow traits.

SHADOW JOURNALING MEDITATION
Use meditation and writing together. Calm your mind with meditation, then write about what you think, feel, or experience. This offers a way to look deeper into yourself and keep track of what you discover.

KINDNESS MEDITATION
Show compassion and kindness to yourself and others. Use affirmations for self-acceptance, embracing your hidden characteristics with kindness and empathy.

SHADOW BLEND MEDITATION
Picture merging your hidden characteristics with your aware self. This type of meditation includes recognizing and accepting the secret parts of you, seeing them blend smoothly with your aware self, promoting a feeling of completeness.

QUIET OBSERVATION MEDITATION
Just sit, quietly noticing thoughts, feelings, and sensations as they come up. Practice detached watching, letting the subconscious aspects of your hidden self come up and fade naturally.

Each kind of meditation gives a unique way to explore and blend aspects. Try out different techniques to find which one clicks with you, exploring your inside world and understanding your hidden self more deeply through shadow work.

Visualization

Shadow work is about understanding our hidden sides. Using our minds, we visualize, or picture these parts of ourselves. This helps us to understand our hidden emotions and patterns better.

In visualization, we create a safe place within our minds. This could be somewhere peaceful like a beach or a forest. Wherever it is, it's a place that feels good to deeply about ourselves. In that mental space, we visualize meeting our shadow self. We might talk to this part of us, letting us understand the emotions and memories it holds.

Visualization helps us look deeper into our subconscious. We see our emotions up close and get insight on things like fear and desire. It's a way to understand parts of ourselves that we cannot understand just by thinking about them. Moreover, visualization is a bridge between our conscious and subconscious. It uses symbols to picture the complex parts of our shadow self. Visualizing these parts helps us to understand and accept them. This brings about better self-awareness and emotional healing.

Remember that when doing shadow work, using your imagination is truly a unique journey. Each person may view it differently due to their own feelings and past encounters. You're not crafting a final, unchangeable image of your hidden self. Instead, you delve into the mysteries of the mind in a manner that clicks with your personal insights.

Shadow work uses different ways of visualizing to have a closer look at the hidden parts of the mind. These are some handy methods:

GUIDED IMAGERY
You can try guided meditation or specific visualization exercises for shadow work. These sessions usually involve a story plot that can help you meet and understand your shadow aspects in a safe place.

INNER DIALOGUE
Picture having a chat with your shadow self. You can be in a coffee shop or any place with a version of you that represents your shadow. It could be like you or something that symbolizes your hidden sides. You converse and listen during this mental dialogue.

SYMBOLIC REPRESENTATION
See the shadow aspects as symbols or creatures or even abstract imageries. For instance, picture the feelings or attributes of the shadow as shapes, colors, or even as unique beings in your inner view.

JOURNEYING VISUALIZATION
Imagine a mental trip in which you set out on an adventure in your mind's landscape. Meet various aspects or scenes of your shadow as you go. This virtual journey lets you study your self's hidden parts.

DREAM WORK VISUALIZATION
When you are about to sleep or while meditating, imagine entering a dream state. In this dream world, you scrutinize scenes or places that stand for your shadow aspects. Notice the symbols, feelings, and encounters that happen. They might give insights from your subconscious.

ART PATH
Have fun by drawing, painting, or crafting pictures of your hidden parts. This lets your mind speak through art, showing new things along the way.

STORY BUILDING
Create a story in your head that shows an adventure of your hidden parts. Imagine you're the main character, going through lessons that teach you about your inside parts.

PEACEFUL IMAGERY
Upon feeling calm, picture a peaceful place in your head. This peaceful place lets you explore your emotions, thoughts, and hidden parts without judgment.

Don't forget that visualizing may work differently for everyone. Try out different methods and see what works best for you. This can help you understand your hidden parts better.

BONUS PAGES

By purchasing this book, you gain access to exclusive bonus content designed to complement your journey through the "Authentic Shadow Work Workbook & Journal For Beginners." This special gift includes guided meditations, visualizations, daily affirmations, and more, all crafted to deepen your understanding and enhance your practice of shadow work. To access your free content, simply scan the QR code at the bottom of this page with your smartphone's camera, and follow the link that appears.

QR

Enjoy this thoughtful addition to your self-discovery journey!

ACTIVITY 2:
Guided Visualization Meditation

Take a few moments to do this short-guided meditation created to learn about your shadow self.

1. Imagine yourself taking a walk down the woods. The sun is bright in the sky and the birds are humming softly.

2. As you walk, your eyes land on a cave nearby. You feel a pull toward it and decide that you will explore it up close.

3. You slowly walk into the cave and are met with a faint light in the distance. You decide to pursue it and find yourself at the door of a room.

4. As you make your way inside the room, you find a mirror. Now, you look into the mirror and look at yourself with fresh eyes. Do you see any shadows or darker parts of yourself that you had been hiding before?

5. Take a deep breath and search for acceptance within yourself. Find the courage to accept those dark parts and imagine them slowly returning to your body and becoming a part of your soul.

6. When you're ready, take a few breaths in and exhale slowly. Bring yourself back to the present moment and open your eyes.

Inner Dialogue

Chatting with your hidden self is a deep shadow work technique. This involves meaningful talks with the parts of you that aren't usually seen. This process helps you connect with these unseen sides of yourself leading to better understanding and acceptance.

THE INNER DIALOGUE PROCESS

BEFORE THE CONVERSATION
First off, find a quiet spot where you can relax. Bring to mind the image of your hidden self– this represents the unseen or unnoticed parts of your mind. It could be an imagined form of you, or a symbol that embodies these elements.

START TALKING
Start the chat by asking questions or simply addressing this hidden self. Let the talk unfold naturally. Ask about feelings, worries, wants, or past experiences tied to these hidden sides. Pay attention to the answers or thoughts that spring up in your mind.

ACTIVE LISTENING AND SEEING
Listen actively without any prejudices or preconceived notions. Notice the answers or feelings that pop up during this symbolic talk. This method promotes kind and nonreactive discussions, encouraging deeper understanding of your hidden sides.

EXPLORING AND ACCEPTING
Use this chat to discover and accept these hidden sides. Ask about the triggers behind certain actions or feelings. Uncover the potential lessons or insights these other sides of you might have. Welcome any feelings or discoveries that come up, understanding and accepting them with kindness.

THE IMPORTANCE OF INNER DIALOGUE

BOOSTED SELF-UNDERSTANDING
Speaking to the shadow self illuminates hidden parts of you. It aids in understanding your motivations, fears, and desires.

EMOTIONAL REPAIR
This method allows for the safe outward expression of trapped emotions or unsettled experiences. It helps with emotional healing.

UNITY AND COMPLETENESS
Talking allows for the combining of shadow parts into the conscious self. This encourages feeling of inner completeness and self-approval.

INSIGHT AND INTROSPECTION
Dialogues with the shadow self provides clarity on personal habits, beliefs, and actions. It enables self-reflection and personal betterment.

Communicating with the shadow self is a deep process that needs an open mind, care, and tolerance. By entering these personal conversations, you can start a journey of self exploration, healing, and fusion. This leads to a profound sense of completeness and self-approval.

Art Therapy

Art therapy serves as a potent means to connect with the repressed aspects of ourselves. It allows us to bring forth unconscious images, which can then be actively experienced, felt, and verbally processed. The realm of creative arts therapy encompasses a wide range of expressive mediums, such as painting, drawing, collage, movement, sound, video, performance art, writing, dreams, and digital media—such as online profiles, choices related to explicit content, avatars, or gaming environments.

Art therapy mixed with shadow work offers a special, silent way to dig into our inner thoughts. People use art to say things they can't put into words. They can directly talk about their feelings and experiences. With shadow work, this art becomes a way for their mind to speak in signs. When people dive into art, they tend to pick certain colors, forms, or pictures. These choices show parts of them they've hidden away. These might be feelings they've pushed down, fights they haven't fixed, or parts of who they are that live in their "shadow self." When they make art, they're actually having a chat with their hidden side. This allows them to bring out and face these hidden parts in a real, touchable way.

Using art to express oneself in shadow work allows exploration of one's inner world and serves as a positive outlet for emotions. It gives a secure, worry free environment where strong emotions or distressing memories can be faced bit by bit. Through involvement in the creative process, people trek their own inner worlds, slowly gaining knowledge of their hidden tendencies and feelings. The artwork created during these sessions becomes a physical thing to study and think about. This helps offer a fresh viewpoint, aiding in gaining a deeper comprehension and acceptance of oneself.

Art therapy helps folks heal and grow, it's like a magic key that unlocks self-expression. By creating something, people can take control of their feelings and experiences. Their inner battles turn into something real something that can see and touch. That's how self-discovery starts. It's how healing begins. It's how the hidden parts of a person become known.

As folks keep creating, they start changing. Slowly but surely, they understand themselves better. They start to accept themselves. They feel more whole. Art isn't just paint and canvas, it's a powerful helper a guide. It helps people on their journey. It brings healing, self-discovery, and unity. The hidden parts get woven into their true selves, making them stronger and more honest.

There are many benefits of art therapy:

FINDING MEANING

Art therapy helps people find meaning in their creations and recognize new aspects of themselves. Discussing with an art therapist and inspecting the symbolism found in their art allows people to understand its meaning. This change process aids in combining the feelings and understandings from their psychedelic encounters into their everyday lives and individual narratives.

AMPLIFIED AWARENESS

Certain forms of art such as abstract painting have the potential to heighten awareness. They can blur the line between a person's conscious and unconscious mind. Taking part in a journey involving art therapy might reveal hidden parts of our shadow self. These parts might have been pushed down or ignored before. The experience can lead to a sense of instability and sometimes fear. Having a skilled Art Therapist on hand, both before and after the experience, can prove really helpful. They can help manage the healing process of these shadow aspects.

EXPRESSIVE OUTLET

Art therapy provides a silent and creative way to express oneself. Through various artistic activities like painting, sketching, molding, or mixed media, people can showcase their inner feelings and thoughts that could have come up during shadow work. This allows the making of tangible displays of unseen parts, encouraging discovery, thoughts, and feeling management.

SYMBOLIC EXPLORATION

Art therapy uses signs and images, which work really well in managing hidden features. By including these signs in their art, people can look at and understand their hidden aspects safely and indirectly. The presence of art symbols helps important self-reflection and make a link between the awake and sleeping mind.

SUPPORT

After doing goal-oriented art, real growth happens. You learn new stuff and you find out if you need to fit it into your day to day life. Using different types of support in addition to art therapy can help you understand your art, manage how you're feeling, and use what you learned to heal over the long term. These supportive techniques include somatic counselling, writing a journal, sacred geometry, and as we've discussed before, meditation.

EXPLORING HIDDEN DEPTHS

Art therapy can support deeper journeys into our subconscious, a part of our mind that's usually hidden. It allows us to understand and reveal hidden emotions, past hurts, and unnoticed patterns of behavior that could affect our health.

HARNESSING EMOTIONS FOR THERAPEUTIC RECOVERY

Art therapy can bring out intense feelings and help to let them go. After people have had this kind of experience, it can help them face and handle tough emotions that came up. This might lead to healing that sticks around for a long time. Sharing who they are through art can work to help them let go of feelings too. When they dive into art, people can sort through and release the tough feelings they have. This helps them understand parts of themselves that they may have been hiding or ignoring. The act of making art gives them a safe place to express these inner feelings.

SPIRITUAL CONNECTION

Art therapy might even boost a personal spiritual connection, ringing in feelings of rising above. It broadens the view, making shadow work more inviting. This bigger picture and deep comprehension lets people explore their own shadow using a spiritual lens.

REFLECTIVE EXPLORATION

Art therapy provides an opportunity for inward reflection and calm mindfulness. The art created mirrors the self, allowing individuals to scrutinize their artistic outputs and uncover hidden feelings and interpretations in the artwork. This journey of contemplation leads to personal realizations, improved self-knowledge, and a deeper understanding of the shadow self.

CREATING A SECURE AND NURTURING ATMOSPHERE

Art therapy meetings generally happen in a safe and caring environment, led by a skilled art therapy professional. This environment cultivates trust, authenticity, and a supportive atmosphere, enabling people to explore and process their intense experiences and internal conflicts. The therapeutic relationship and direction from the art therapy professional are crucial in offering helpful support throughout the process of integration.

EMPOWERMENT AND SELF-DISCOVERY

Art therapy allows people to take an active role in their own wellness and self-exploration. By diving into creativity, they gain a sense of control and responsibility. This involves discovering and understanding their inner, hidden experiences.

5. DREAM ANALYSIS: DECIPHERING THE LANGUAGE OF UNCONSCIOUS

Dreams help unlock the complicated areas of our mind hidden in shadow work. In the dream world, our quiet mind uses symbols, comparisons, and coded messages. This place stores feelings that we don't talk about, fears, wants, and pushed down past situations, showing parts of our mind that we might miss when awake. Dreams display our personal struggles, unanswered problems, and overlooked parts about us metaphorically, giving a special look into our quieter mind's depths.

Dream symbols are like complicated puzzles, revealing parts of our hidden selves. We might see some things over again, like important characters or new places. All of these have deep meaning. The things that we see in dreams often align with our own inner conflicts. They open up a window into the parts of us that we've pushed away, not accepted, or kept out of our direct knowing. In all these symbols, there are a bunch of clues to put together. These clues give us a guide to get through the twisted paths of our own minds.

In dream analysis, we start an adventure to discover and explain, aiming to decode hidden meanings in these visions we get. Looking beyond the obvious into dream symbols and understanding their personal meaning unlocks broader knowledge of our subconscious mind. Feelings encountered in dreams act as markers, leading us toward uncharted areas of our inner space, letting us face unaddressed emotions, fears, or past hurts that resonate within our inner shadows.

On top of all that, understanding dreams isn't just about interpreting lone symbols. It's about pulling these pieces together to form a clear story that mirrors our real world life. This helps us connect our awake and dreaming minds, bringing the lessons of our dreams into everyday awareness. This weaving in strengthens our self-understanding, helping to confront and accept our inner darkness. Through this, dreams become a deep resource for self-knowledge, emotional repair, and smoothly joining together the different layers of our minds.

The Process Of Dream Analysis

Analyzing dreams for shadow work is a streamlined method. It digs into the symbolic language of dreams, untangles their secret symbolism and combines them into our day to day awareness.

DREAM RECALL

Right after you wake up, record your dream into a journal before it fades away. Write down all the details you can remember—clear pictures, feelings, prominent symbols, people, locations, and behaviors. This quick logging safekeeps the core of your dream before it slips away from your memory.

RECOGNIZING SIGNS AND REPEATING PATTERNS

Look into your dreams carefully for repeating themes, signs, or feelings. Often, signs in dreams mirror our hidden thoughts, showing parts of us or feelings that we might ignore or forget when we're awake. Watch for any repeating signs or themes, because they are often important hints to the masked parts we need to examine.

PERSONAL CONNECTIONS

Think about the personal meanings behind the symbolism that shows up in your dreams. Reflect on how these signs can be related to your everyday life. Look into how they make you feel and how they connect to previous experiences or issues that you haven't solved yet. Examine how these signs match up with your inner feelings and emotions. This will reveal parts of your shadow self.

EXPLORING EMOTIONS

Look into the emotions felt during the dream. Emotions are strong signs that can highlight hidden feelings or bottled up emotions inside your shadow self. Keep an eye on the strength, type, and setting of these emotions. They offer useful hints within the spaces of self-discovery and recovery.

REFLECTION

Reflect on how your dreams relate to your awake life. Think about how the symbols or feelings from the dream link to your day to day thoughts, actions, or feelings. This type of reflection promotes a much deeper understanding of your shadow self.

This method to understand dreams for shadow work offers a way to interpret the coded meanings hidden in the detailed patterns of our dreams. It helps us know our inner world better and aids us in observing and reconnecting with our shadow self.

Benefits Of Dream Analysis

Analyzing dreams is really important in shadow work. It has many advantages and helps us understand and heal ourselves better.

SYMBOLIC INSIGHTS

Dreams use symbols, like a picture showing what's inside us. By looking at these symbols, we can understand hidden thoughts from our unspoken parts. Dream symbols are like secret messages that tell us truths about our secret self, helping us know parts of us that might be hidden or mixed up when we're awake.

UNCONSCIOUS PROCESSING

Dreams offer a stage for the hidden part of our mind to handle feelings, experiences, and issues that might not come up in our day to day thoughts. Looking into dreams works like a link connecting our daily thoughts and our hidden ones, leading these unnoticed aspects to come out. By untangling the secret meanings, people can get to deep feelings or problems, helping them become aware and understand their hidden parts.

HEALING AND RESOLUTION

Breaking down the hidden messages in our dreams helps our emotional recovery and problem solving. Dreams tend to expose unresolved feelings, worries or arguments that live in our hidden self. By recognizing and dealing with these parts exposed during dream evaluation, people start a growth process. This leads to emotional recovery, solving internal fights, and brings a feeling of internal calm and equilibrium.

SELF-EXPLORATION AND INTERGRATION

Studying dreams leads to inner examination and self-learning. This helps you spotlight parts of you that might go unnoticed or be pushed down. It acts like a mirror, helping combine hidden parts into clear knowledge. Looking at the signs and feelings in dreams, people go on a self-finding trip. This nourishes a deeper recognizing and approval of their complex inner world.

Therefore, analyzing dreams as part of shadow work is a strong method for discovering the hidden parts of the subconscious mind. It lets people delve into, mend, and blend their shadow sides. This leads to significant personal development, increased self-understanding, and smoothly brings together the various parts of the mind.

ACTIVITY 3:
Dream Recall and Record

Think about your last dream for a moment. Pick the thing/person/place that feels the most vibrant. What was most memorable? It could be an odd item, something scary, or a really strong image. Spend some time thinking hard about this. Maybe even draw it, if drawing's your thing.

Next, keeping in mind your identity as the object, answer the following six questions:

As a

1. My Purpose Is

2. My Goal Is

3. My Biggest Fear Is

4. I Love

5. I Hate

6. I Desire/Wish

6.
THE POWER OF POSITIVITY
HARNESSING AFFIRMATIONS IN SHADOW WORK

Positive affirmations have a varied role in shadow work. They're powerful tools for self-healing and transformation. Positive affirmations help counteract subconscious patterns in shadow work. They interfere with old thought habits that can cause feelings of fear or self-doubt. Using affirmations carefully helps people to bravely accept themselves, feel empowered, and start healing. This, in turn, begins a process of rewiring the subconscious mind. Old or unhelpful beliefs slowly lose place to supportive and encouraging thoughts. This brain change helps people feel better about themselves. It fosters a stronger sense of self-worth.

Using positive statements daily helps people develop a mindset needed for shadow work. This mindset includes accepting oneself, being strong, and being open. These positive statements act like guiding stars. They steer us toward positive change and growth. They also support a caring environment for uniting shadow aspects with the conscious self.

Affirmations: More Than Just Positive Thoughts

Analyzing dreams for shadow work is a streamlined method. It digs into the symbolic language of dreams, untangles their secret symbolism and combines them into our day to day awareness.

Positive affirmations are affirmations that involve expressing positive statements about oneself. They are always written in the first person, in the present tense, and presented as if they were true for the person at the present moment. The purpose of positive affirmations is to create a positive mindset and reinforce positive beliefs about oneself. These affirmations can be used in various contexts, such as personal development, self-improvement, and maintaining a positive attitude in daily life.

Positive affirmations encompass statements like, "I possess the capability to achieve any goal I dedicate myself to," "I exhibit the bravery required to pursue my aspirations," and "I embrace self-acceptance in my current state."

Once you genuinely embrace and incorporate positive affirmations, their impact can be transformative. Positive affirmations possess the ability to replace a negative inner dialogue with a positive one, enhancing self-confidence and sparking inspiration. Consequently, they facilitate the transition from mere thoughts to concrete actions in your everyday life, beyond the realm of your mind.

You might be skeptical about the effectiveness of positive affirmations. How can saying positive statements bring about significant and enduring changes in our deeply ingrained thought patterns?

You are right to a certain extent. Merely stating the affirmations isn't enough. In order for affirmations to be effective, it is crucial to have even a small level of belief in what you are saying. Let's consider the affirmation "I am a money magnet" as an example. While you may not currently believe this affirmation to be true, it is important to be open to the potential for it to become true. You should be willing to cultivate your belief and strengthen your conviction in order for these words to resonate with you on a deeper level.

Regarding the science behind affirmations working successfully, brain flexibility, crucial in neuroscience, points to the brain's knack for reshaping due to thoughts and experiences. Investigations using brain imaging tools, such as fMRI, indicate that regular positive sentiments can stir brain areas connected with rewards and self-related processing. These experiments show that positive statements lead to shifts in brain activity and connections, highlighting the brain's ability to adapt and create new nerve routes based on consistent positive thinking.

Psychology delves into how affirmations impact our self-image and actions. The self-affirmation theory, born from social psychologists, underscores affirming personal core beliefs for maintaining self-respect. Studies show affirmations can safeguard against self-esteem threats, lessen stress reactions, and boost problem solving skills. For example, research discovered that people practicing self-affirmation show heightened self-esteem and a brighter outlook.

Research on how affirmations affect behavior has shown good outcomes. It's been observed in health behavior studies, like stopping smoking or eating better, that using affirmations can boost motivation. Also, in school settings, it appears affirmations connect to better grades, sticking with it, and toughness in students who are dealing with hard situations.

Although affirmations aren't quick solutions, research shows they can gradually change our thoughts, feelings, and behaviors. This growing proof points to affirmations' ability to reform beliefs, boost self-image, and alter actions. The blend of psychology and neuroscience lays a sturdy base for affirmations' use in enhancing ourselves, progressing personally, and promoting wellness.

Furthermore, as with the majority of aspects in life, in order to achieve significant advancements, one must demonstrate dedication and consistently engage in the practice of affirmations. Just as a plant requires daily sunlight and water to flourish and develop, positive affirmations require regular reflection and repetition for their growth.

Mastering The Art Of Positive Affirmations

To deepen and reinforce our faith and confidence in affirmations, it is essential that we actively interact with them in various ways. We must consciously engage with each affirmation, addressing any negative thoughts or resistance that arise.

HARNESS THE POWER OF AUDIO RECORDINGS FOR POSITIVE SELF-TALK

If you're looking for an effective and straightforward method to begin incorporating positive affirmations into your life, consider exploring audio recordings. You'll find a wide array of options on the internet, with YouTube serving as a great starting point.

Audio recordings have the remarkable advantage of being effortlessly incorporated into a hectic daily schedule. You can conveniently play these recordings in the background while engaging in various activities such as driving, cooking, bathing, falling asleep, or even while going for a walk or jog. Their flexibility allows for seamless integration into numerous aspects of your daily routine.

CRAFT AND CAPTURE PERSONALLY EMPOWERING AFFIRMATIONS

While it is beneficial to listen to recordings made by others, it is more advantageous to generate and record your own distinctive set of affirmative statements. This should be tailored to your circumstances, as well as the specific objectives and results you aspire to achieve. By personalizing our efforts and making them unique to our individual requirements, we can maximize the benefits we derive from this undertaking.

PHYSICAL ACTIVITIES AND EMPOWERING SELF-TALK

Combining exercise with positive affirmations can elevate things to another level. By merging physical activity and affirmative statements, we acquire the capability to connect our constructive affirmations with the heightened sensations of well-being and joy that exercise elicits.

THE POWER OF YIN YOGA AND UPLIFTING SELF-TALK

Incorporating positive affirmations into yin yoga poses is an innovative approach developed by Kassandra Reinhardt. According to her, as we progressively stretch and expand our physical body, we also gain a more profound connection with our emotional, mental, and spiritual being. It is widely believed among yoga enthusiasts that emotions have a physical presence in the body. By practicing specific stretches that target the areas where painful or suppressed emotions are believed to be stored, it is believed that these emotions can be released, benefiting both the physical and mental well-being.

When we incorporate yin yoga positions with the practice of positive affirmations, we are simultaneously addressing our emotions on both a mental and physical level.

To illustrate, let's consider the affirmation "I attract wealth effortlessly." During the practice of yin yoga, you have the opportunity to repeatedly affirm positive statements internally. It is important to pay attention to the effect these affirmations have on your emotions. Is your belief in yourself as a money magnet genuine? Does this affirmation elicit positive emotions when spoken? Alternatively, does it trigger feelings of anxiety, tension, or fear? If the affirmation provokes negative thoughts and emotions, it indicates the need for further introspection and exploration to determine its underlying causes.

ACTIVITY 4:
Beginner-Friendly Affirmations

Say each affirmation five times and try to practice them daily.

- [ ] I am open to journeying into the depths of my hidden self.

- [ ] I have trust in my process of self-exploration.

- [ ] I am letting go of fear and embracing the knowledge my shadows disclose.

- [ ] My shadows hold insightful information about my personal growth.

- [ ] I wholeheartedly accept and understand all parts of me.

- [ ] My shadows aren't shortcomings but rather a gateway to growth.

- [ ] I approach my shadows with an open mind and heart.

- [ ] Every part of my shadow work will aid my healing journey.

- [ ] I am forgiving myself for any judgments I make against my shadows.

- [ ] I am gaining more awareness of the patterns in my feelings and actions.

- [ ] Delving into shadow work is allowing me to reunite with my true self.

☐ I trust that shadow work will lead me to greater self-awareness.

☐ I am letting go of urge for perfection and am owning my imperfections.

☐ My shadows aren't hurdles, they are stepping stones to self-discovery.

☐ I am kind and gentle toward myself as I practice shadow work.

☐ I am choosing growth over comfort in my voyage of self-discovery.

☐ Each shadow work activity will get me closer to inner peace.

☐ I am strong, and I can take on and learn from my shadows.

☐ I welcome the chance to reveal the depths of my authentic self.

☐ Owning my shadows will lead to a peaceful and fulfilling life.

7. NAVIGATING THROUGH EMOTIONAL WAVES

Diving into self-reflective activities demands a substantial level of emotional courage. It calls for uncovering and accepting elements of ourselves that have been neglected before.

Giving them space to exist and recognizing their existence welcomes in rays of new viewpoints to our darkness and promotes a more profound understanding. This exercise is extremely subtle and is devoid of any flair, glitter, or pleasure. It necessitates acknowledging and tackling our own fears, insecurities, humiliation, jealousy, fury, egotism, biases, criticisms, and suffering.

Exploring shadow work can be deeply humbling. It's a journey that can be quite heavy, even knocking you off your balance sometimes. It means diving deep into your most severe wounds, peeling away the layers of your deepest injuries. Even though it's tough, it also has a beautiful side, leading the way for major soul growth. It's a transformational expedition, similar to undergoing a metamorphosis.

Even with life looking hard, we always have choices. Either we can keep our pain hidden, making more darkness. Or, we can take on the real feelings that come up during tough times, seeing them as part of who we are. Going through these hard times leads us to our deepest troubles. This gives us the chance to face and deal with them.

Facing and acknowledging all parts of ourselves that we've previously overlooked is important. This shift in self-perception affects how we see others too. When we stop ignoring aspects of our character, we stop attributing these features to others and this stops us from disregarding them. This results in relationships being more effortless, deep and worthwhile. You lift your spiritual self to a higher level and welcome new, varied people into your life. Shadow work will always exist. Don't let it scare you. Instead, welcome it and give up control.

Types Of Discomfort That Come With Shadow Work

Pain comes in different types: in your mind, body, or feelings. Mental troubles might pop up when hard to digest information comes our way, or stuff that we struggle to recall. Body hurts may show themselves when we strain ourselves to the max, helping us get stronger. Heartache might come around when we face off the scary aspects of ourselves, battling to loosen their hold on how we live.

Growth needs discomfort to happen. Think, if we were happy with a bad job, would we want to learn more? Also, if being lazy made us fit, would we bother to work out? And, would a young bird leave its nest if it didn't feel too crowded and dirty inside?

Pain grabs our focus, pulling it from unnoticed thoughts, signals in our body, or our surroundings. It points out a need for shift, a need to mend an injury, a warning of risk, or the workings of the muscle being made stronger.

By trying new things and learning from our past, we increase our understanding of ourselves and our aim in life. Going through tough times helps us build our skills and develop confidence. Like a tree getting stronger with each gust of wind, we can create a solid foundation to raise our goals high. As we understand that our muscles increase only through hard exercises and not by staying comfortable, our mental and spiritual abilities also bloom when exposed to difficulties.

The self aims to keep us alive but without focus, we may be stuck in fight or flight. Therefore, the self naturally puts us in the heart of things, seeking to manage situations and steer clear of trouble. Our progress and changes teach us that we can't improve or evolve without facing hardships, just like we can't have daytime without nighttime.

When faced with tough feelings, we often dodge them. We find distractions, numb ourselves, chase quick joys, or calm ourselves. Yet, by this, we lose our shot to rise and reach a grander state of mind. Instead of struggling to manage people and our conditions, we should alter how we react. See the problems from the world as chances and gifts, not as penalties.

Looking after yourself means being kind to yourself. This involves talking nicely to ourselves and treating ourselves well. One important thing is to become our own biggest supporter so we can be the best we can be. Sometimes, life gives us serious pain in certain areas. During these tough times, it's crucial to be gentle with ourselves everywhere else. This can mean leaning on our friends and family for comfort during sad times. Or it may mean giving our bodies extra care and nourishment when we're feeling sick.

Each person who's mastered self-strength knows how crucial it is to accept the uneasy. It is by facing obstacles with kindness, not dread, that our deepest skills show up. By treating our fears as mirrors, we slowly expose our real selves and move big steps toward formerly unreachable goals. As we boldly start this makeover trip, our better selves cheer, realizing they've handed us the secret to self-advancement. Our only job is to say yes to this invaluable prize.

Strategies For Handling Emotional Discomfort

Going through tough emotions in shadow work calls for tactics to handle and work through these feelings. This is key for a helpful and rewarding journey.

UNDERSTANDING EMOTIONS
Develop mindfulness by noticing and observing feelings without forming opinions. Let yourself remain with these feelings, recognizing their existence without attempting to bottle up or overly attach with them.

BREATHING AND CALMING METHODS
Doing deep breath exercises or calming methods will help stay present. Techniques such as square breathing or paying attention to body feelings can handle feelings and bring peace.

KEEP A JOURNAL
Record your feelings, happenings, and realizations as you do shadow work. Writing about what's on your mind helps clear it and lower emotional stress. This helps you reflect and understand more deeply.

BE KIND TO YOURSELF
Show yourself some kindness and warmth. Understand that sometimes feeling uneasy is just part of life's journey. Give yourself the same sympathy and comprehension you would provide a buddy who's going through a tough time.

GET HELP
Connect with a dependable friend, counselor, or group. Chat about your experiences and feelings with those who comprehend or offer an impartial space. This can give a sense of approval and clarity.

MAKE A SAFE SPACE
Set up a peaceful place for shadow work. Utilize calming traditions or items, like relaxing tunes, candles, or pleasant smells, to build a safe and caring environment for discovery.

WELLNESS STRATEGIES
Place importance on self-care tasks that help with resting and feeling good. Things like working out, quiet reflection, enjoying the outdoors, or taking part in fun hobbies.

MAKE RULES
Understand when to pause or back off if feelings get too strong. Making rules for your shadow work routine helps you to participate at a speed that's comfortable for you.

EXPERT ADVICE
Think about asking for help from a therapist or counselor who knows about shadow work. They can give you customized plans and backup to handle strong feelings and tricky parts of the process.

Keep in mind that feeling uneasy is a normal piece of shadow work. By using these techniques, you build a helpful structure to manage and merge these feelings. This promotes growth and self-understanding throughout this transformation journey.

Understanding when to take a break from shadow work is also crucial for self-care and emotional balance. But, how do we know when to pause? One sure signal is when feelings become too strong and interfere with daily life. This happens when emotions become too much, causing stress. It's a sign that we need to reset emotionally. Also, if you're always tired or have symptoms like headaches or troubled sleep, it could mean that the emotional work is taking a toll. So, these are signs that we need physical rest and recovery.

Moreover, when exploring shadows becomes stagnant, overly complex, or not making sense, it shows that we need to pause. A strong desire to steer clear from shadow work may display possible exhaustion. It's urgent to stop and refill our emotional tank. Ignoring self-care, seeing yourself suffer due to strong emotions, or observing the negative effects it has on relationships and friends points out the desperation to value our self-kindness and health above all.

Listen to your gut. When a feeling of being overloaded, uneasy, or overly emotional pops up, it means you should take some time off. Accept these times as normal. This lets you respect your emotional needs. Then you can refocus and jump back into the deep personal exploration when you are ready. Taking breaks isn't about failing. It shows a deep understanding of self-care and handling emotions while you explore your inner self.

Dealing With Fear Of Facing Painful Emotions

Fear is a mental state, born from strong beliefs about oneself and the world. Beating fear isn't just about changing your point of view. It's about questioning a hidden belief that sees the fear as undeniable fact. Your body learns to agree with this, even if it may not match real life.

When we're deep in our own thoughts, we often see our current situation through those thoughts. This means our minds often act like they need to protect us. We see things not related to us as possibly harmful. This happens without us realizing, even if there's no real danger around us. But our bodies react like we're in big danger anyway. This is why we're scared a lot. It's linked to the natural need to stay safe. It makes us want to fight, run away, or freeze up.

Think about feeling scared of judgment. This fear can come about in different ways. For me, it shows up when I'm doing my spiritual practices, and my family, who isn't spiritual, is there. I feel like they're silently judging my lifestyle choice. The fear grows bigger in my mind, thinking things like "They don't accept me," "They believe I'm odd," "Why can't I be like everyone else?" These thoughts repeat nonstop, feeding the fear. In response, my body goes into alarm mode: "We're not okay!" "This is scary!" "We may not survive!" These scared thoughts cause physical reactions like hands sweating, heart pounding, thoughts running, and I'm overcome with anxiety and hardship.

When you're scared, it typically suggests that while you're actually safe, you're simply not comfortable. Being safe and feeling comfortable aren't always the same. To conquer your fears, you ought to teach your mind to understand that feeling uneasy doesn't always signal danger. This practice lets you tackle life with an attitude of progress and creativity instead of just plain survival.

By choosing to have a creative approach, you place yourself in a position to actively make improved decisions, free from the regular unrest and worry that often come with instinctive choices. Instead of feeling swamped and uneasy, your reactions originate from a zone of calm and internal steadiness.

Beating fear isn't an easy or fast job. It involves tweaking how you think and altering how your body responds to scares. If you look at fear with an energy viewpoint, it's seen as stuck, low-level energy that has been in your body since it started. When you let go of fear, you spot this low-level energy and allow it to escape via your emotional outlet. Letting out feelings in an energy manner may appear as tears, or if you're upset, maybe you choose to toss out the energy through an intense workout.

In survival mode, particularly during reactions like fight, flight, or freeze, fear energy isn't properly discharged. This causes stagnant energy to build up. As fear keeps getting sparked, the low frequency energy in our bodies starts to grow. This is similar to "sweeping it under the rug"—the fear doesn't go away. As a result, the fear's intensity grows over time. This isn't because the situations outside are getting worse, but because of the growing internal energy.

Your worry springs from a strong conviction you've carried for a lengthy period. When we look closely, it's clear that this thought frequently emerges out of feeling not enough or lacking self-value. To beat your fears, you should look into what causes them and how they stem from your central beliefs.

Understanding how fear links to our feelings connects directly to the next stage of dealing with and working through discomfort. Basically, these steps often go hand in hand in the big picture.

Overcoming fear includes spotting and facing your inner fear energy. When in a survival state, we see the world in a skewed way and naturally respond to things that may harm us.

Facing fear involves learning to handle the tied up pain and emotions. By truly letting these feelings in, you get rid of the energy that powers your fear. At first, meeting fear might have been hard. This is because it sparked a knee jerk response: either to fight, run away, or freeze up. But, as you dig through your fear and choose on purpose to let it go, you make a safe space. Here, you can reassure yourself you're safe. You can also completely accept your feelings.

Nervousness around feeling our emotions can be harder than actually recognizing and working through them. The world around you can often spark fear as you don't control it. Yet, by actively letting go of fear and striving for peace inside, we recognize that we can control our inner state.

To beat fear, find a new and uplifting thought that matches your dreams. This method makes sure that when fear pops up later, you can notice the unease but tell yourself you are safe right now. Besides, use this encouraging belief to spark optimism and move ahead.

This potent view nudges you to move from just getting by to actively shaping. If you stick to just getting by, you'll always feel like life's events are just hitting you. But, shaping allows you to recognize your fear and uneasiness, telling yourself that fear is normal, and it doesn't mean you're in danger. You purposely decide to breathe through the fear, reminding yourself it doesn't dictate your value. By consciously making this choice, you take back control over your fear, stopping it from ruling your actions.

Shaking off your fear needs constant work and dedication to adjust your lifestyle. This isn't an overnight transformation but a slow process requiring commitment and time. You have the inner power to uplift yourself and grasp optimism. Although there might be instances when you slip back into dread, always remember the methodical strategy to let go of the dark energy tied with fear and come back to a place of optimism and care.

ACTIVITY 5:
Fear Flow Exercise

Give this physical activity a shot to relate to the core of your fear. Even though it's not about removing or conquering the fear, many times, addressing your fear through physical actions can lessen it.

Where's my body holding this fear today?

....

....

Fear often appears in your body as tightness, trembling, quicker heart rate, alterations in your usual breathing, or fidgeting. It's totally normal if your fear manifests in other ways too.

What is this fear like in my body?

....

....

Get eager to learn. Don't judge it in any way. Observe its attributes like you're describing to a person.

What's happening now?

....

....

It might sound odd, but it's now time to embrace the fear in your body more fiercely.

Take deep breaths and tap the part of your body that holds fear five times.

As you move or breathe, keep a curious mind and question yourself "what's going on now?" about every half minute to minute.

Stay with the sensations and feelings that come up. Observe them calmly. Try your best to let what you notice exist without making any efforts to alter the experience.

When To Get Professional Help

Getting help from an expert for shadow work is important when trying to manage it by yourself seems too difficult. Knowing about shadow work is good, but there are times when you really need expert advice.

Strong feelings can greatly affect one's well-being in shadow work, so having some expert guidance important. When emotions become too powerful or continually disturb everyday life, leading to discomfort, worry, or sadness, it's essential to reach out to a therapist with shadow work experience. These emotions, often found during the examination of the shadow self, can be significant, erupting unhandled problems, hidden traumas, or held back feelings that may seem hard to handle without professional assistance.

A shadow work therapist sets up a sheltered, organized space to make sense of deep feelings. They offer a place where folks can freely talk about their feelings. With specific therapy methods like strategies that change behavior, exercises that focus attention, or treatments that know about trauma, they help individuals handle these feelings. They guide people to understand these feelings as a part of themselves.

Also, counselors who know shadow work can show people their routine, triggers, or deep reasons of emotional pain. They help a strong grasp of feelings within the shadow's context, leading people toward accepting themselves and recovery. By digging into where tough emotions come from, therapists aid in changing these strong feelings into useful knowledge and chances for improvement.

Therapists give helpful tools to control feelings and deal with tough emotional situations well. By using custom aid, folks master good ways to cope, ways to control emotions, and calming practices. These are used to deal with strong emotions that may come up when doing the complex task of shadow work.

Cracking into our inner thoughts during shadow work can dig up deep wounds and unresolved problems. This requires expert therapy. Handling this type of hurt needs a kind and organized approach from a counselor who knows about trauma care. These pros are great at leading us through tough emotional paths, providing a safe spot for recovery and change.

Trauma trained therapists establish a safe, structured area where people can delve into past traumas or ingrained issues without fear of re traumatization. Their toolbox includes specific methods like trauma centered treatments (think EMDR or Somatic Experiencing), sharing stories, and mindfulness exercises designed for healing trauma. These techniques nurture slow, tender examination of traumatic memories, granting people the space to understand and accept these experiences in their own time.

In other words, therapists with trauma informed care skills focus on promoting safety, empowerment, and trust in therapy. They guide people into building good stress busting techniques and emotional control methods. This way, they help manage the emotional roller coaster usually present in trauma treatment.

In trauma aware counseling, the focus lies in forming an equal and power sharing environment, which values a person's freedom and timing. These counselors aid in reshaping distressing events, building strength, and helping to regain a feeling of security and control.

By seeking advice from trauma therapists, people doing shadow work can understand trauma recovery and mix these experiences into their self-understanding journey. This specific help offers a detailed and kind structure, encouraging a more whole and healing look at the shadow self.

Diving into shadow work, you might hit a wall, feel confused, or not move forward. It can be tough and puzzling. It helps to get an expert therapist who knows about shadow work during these difficult times because they have useful advice and methods. They can steer you the right way again and help you make progress. They can help break new ground in your understanding and growth.

Counselors skilled in shadow work give a special viewpoint and direction. This helps people better understand their minds' intricate layers. They offer a new viewpoint to look into things that just aren't moving. Often, they reveal unseen parts or trends that block the way forward. Their expert knowledge helps find the root cause of problems, triggers, or unaddressed issues. These are things that add to the sense of not being able to move forward in their journey.

In a nutshell, therapists use particular methods tailored to shadow work. They provide tailored plans and activities aimed to spark self-discovery, nurture self-thought, and reignite forward movement in the process. By using methods like analyzing dreams, talking with your shadow self, or exploring narratives, therapists nudge people to delve deeper. This helps foster a more profound understanding of the shadow aspects.

As the exploration of one's subconscious progresses, situations might arise where thoughts or actions regarding self-harm or suicidal ideation could surface. Quick professional help must be sought. Such mindsets or actions hint at a pressing requirement for support and assistance. It is necessary to reach out to mental health experts, emergency hotlines, or emergency service providers to guarantee the safety and welfare of the person having such thoughts or actions. These experts can provide urgent help, support, and direction to manage these grave instances and uphold the person's safety.

Turning to experts for assistance in these vital times ensures that folks get the required support, instruction, and attention to journey through the trials of shadow work in a secure and practical manner.

8. DEALING WITH SHADOW WORK REACTIONS

Knowing what causes reactions is extremely important in the area of shadow work. They are like doorways to deep understanding and development. Triggers, although they can be quiet, have huge effects. They bring to light hidden parts of us that exist in our subconscious. These are emotional or behavioral hints that cause strong responses, showing where untouched hurts, unsettled feelings, or pushed down parts of ourselves lie.

Recognizing Your Triggers

In the process of shadow work, noticing these triggers effectively becomes a helpful guide, steering focus toward undiscovered parts of the mind that need investigation and blending. By pinpointing what prompts strong emotional reactions—like anger, fear, sadness, or discomfort—one unlocks insights into the hidden shadow features. These triggers often reflect unrecognized portions of oneself, giving a chance for self-reflection and comprehension.

Indeed, pinpointing triggers lets people better steer their emotions. This presents an opportunity to stop, ponder, and dig into why these responses occur. By examining themselves, people discover trends, thoughts, or past happenings that cause these triggers, simplifying a profound comprehension of their psyche.

Also, recognizing what upsets us forms a link between what we know and don't know about ourselves, starting a chat with our hidden side. By facing these upsets, people start a change process, giving hidden feelings and parts of themselves a chance to show and be reviewed and eventually merge.

Triggers are like guides. They point people to parts of themselves that need care and insight. These triggers usually come from past happenings, feelings that haven't been dealt with, social molding, or hidden beliefs. They stand for parts of oneself that have been pushed to the background. They pop up out of nowhere, sparking strong feelings or habits that may seem too much for what's going on right now.

By being mindful of one's reactions, folk can dig into their minds. These episodes of strong feelings reveal hidden parts of oneself. Tucked away traumas, not yet processed feelings, or buried wants and thoughts are exposed. The unease sparked by such powerful reactions invites us to look into these hidden parts, to begin healing and acceptance.

Identifying what sets us off is a key instance for self-examination and exploration. It spurs people to probe into the hidden causes for their actions, promoting a better grasp of the ideas, scares, or doubts that spur these reactions. This inward scrutiny sheds light on entrenched ways of acting or thinking, enabling folks to free themselves from these programmed reactions.

Surely, recognizing what inspires action allows room for informed decisions and an enhanced sense of control. Instead of acting on impulse, people have the ability to reply in a mindful manner. Increasing their understanding of self helps them handle situations that may provoke their feelings in a smarter way, lessening extreme emotional responses and increasing emotional strength.

In the end, noticing triggers is vital in shadow work because it encourages us to face and accept our "shadow" side knowingly. It opens up a road to learning about ourselves, healing, and growing, setting the stage for a more united, truthful, and free life. By respecting and examining triggers, we start on a journey to increased self-knowledge, emotional recovery, and a broader comprehension of the complex web of our inner emotions.

Watching how you respond is a key part of shadow work. It gives a strong path to knowing and bringing together the unseen parts of yourself. Reactions, either feelings or actions, typically act as hints. These often reveal hidden shadow components deep within the subconscious mind.

In shadow work, we learn to view our reactions from a distance. Instead of reacting instantly, we step back. We witness our thoughts, feelings, and actions. There's no judgment, no attachment. Just a careful observer watching our reactions take shape.

This habit helps people understand the hidden parts of their minds. If you pay attention to unexpected feelings—like quick anger, unnecessary guard, or intense emotions—you can find what pushes your buttons. These feelings often show parts of ourselves we don't admit. They spotlight feelings we haven't dealt with, wounds that haven't healed, or characteristics we ignore.

Also, watching reactions promotes understanding ourselves deeper. It paves the way for thinking, allowing people to ponder why they respond in certain ways. This exploration into oneself reveals more about our minds, helping to recognize habits, mental molding, or past instances leading to these reactions.

Moreover, this method promotes a feeling of stepping back from automatic reactions. By watching reactions without criticism, people can put a space between the trigger and the reaction. This lets us take more calculated, considered actions instead of just reacting on impulse. This fresh pause gives the chance to consciously choose our response, instead of just following subconscious habits.

ACTIVITY 6:
Three, Two, One

This exercise blends different shadow work methods into a three-step activity. It's fantastic for assisting you with a trigger, or to manage a situation that triggers you.

Begin by thinking about the situation; in this instance, select a person/place/object who you struggle to be with/in because it causes feelings of distress.

3. FACE IT

The first step is confronting your reaction source.

Picture the source of distress in your thoughts —form a crisp mental image of it, then start thinking about everything you feel being around it.

Begin to note down the things in them that stir negative emotions in you. Maybe it's the color of an object, the voice of a person, or the lighting of a particular space.

2. TALK TO IT

The next phase involves interacting with this stressor in your mind. You aren't actually conversing with the thing. Instead, you engage in "internal dialogue" and say whatever is on your mind. Yell at it, scold it, accept it.

Speak up, jot it down, or just ponder on it do what suits you best. Share the way that this thing makes you feel.

1. BE IT

The last part is the toughest. You must become the person, place or thing you've been reflecting on. Picture being them and expressing all the traits you've noted as though you're talking about yourself. "I am arrogant. I am self-important" and so on.

This part helps with exposing those characteristics, letting you confront them instead of hiding or pinning them on others.

Unveiling Hidden Patterns

How we view and understand life events is mostly shaped by what we believe. This concept is a crucial part of a method known as Rational Emotive Behavior Therapy (REBT). This zeroes in on the idea that what we think, feel, and do are all linked to one another, impacting our overall health and happiness. Let's take a look at a few examples:

THE ICEBERG MODEL

This model is like a mystery that explains human behavior. Picture it as an iceberg in the sea—only a small portion is visible, while a large part remains unseen. According to Sigmund Freud, "The unconscious mind is the primary source of human behavior. Like an iceberg, the most important part of the mind is the part you cannot see" (*The Unconscious*, 1915). People's actions may appear straightforward, but there's often more to it. What we see is just a small piece. This model helps us reveal the true motives hidden underneath.

WHAT'S ON THE SURFACE?

When we look at people, we see their actions, words, and faces. Like if someone is mad, we notice the anger. But there may be deeper feelings hidden under that anger. Maybe fear. Or maybe issues from the past. We might miss these if we only see what's on the surface.

WHAT'S HIDDEN BELOW?

In the depths of the mind, mysteries await exploration. These include secret elements like personal beliefs, past experiences, carried emotions, cultural heritage, self-image, and life aspirations. These ingredients blend into why individuals act as they do.

WHY IT'S IMPORTANT

Grasping the Iceberg Model enhances our day to day existence. It improves our communication skills, mitigates confusions, and prompts introspection. It fosters empathy and comprehension. If setbacks emerge, it empowers us to delve deeper and not limit ourselves to surface level resolution.

The Iceberg Model helps us decode the unseen factors influencing people's actions. Recognizing that actions are influenced by hidden factors can enhance our interactions, avoid confusion, and provide better self-understanding. It nurtures empathy and effective problem solving. Digging deeper into both ourselves and others sparks personal development and improves relationships.

BEHAVIORS AS CLUES

What we do can often uncover what we feel or think. Picture a friend who loves hanging out, but now dodges social scenes. They might be wrestling with sadness or worry. Imagine a person who's always on time but now is often tardy or skips commitments. Likely, they're drowning in pressure or feeling swamped. Such behavior shifts hint at a deeper turmoil churning within their emotional or mental state.

Knowing how our actions are formed is essential. They're not solely based on our mind and emotions, but also elements like our surroundings and past incidents. For instance, consider a person who had a negative encounter with dogs before, they could create an intense fear of dogs, steering clear of them entirely. Here, their previous encounter greatly shapes their present actions.

When you take notice of what you do and how it ties to your thinking and emotions, you start to spot routines. You can pinpoint what sparks off harmful negative thoughts and emotions. Grasping this concept is key to good mental health and well-being. This fundamental thought is the center of REBT, where individuals learn to question and modify unhelpful thinking. This leads to happier feelings and actions.

ACTIVITY 7:
Three Steps to Recognize Your Self-Sabotaging Patterns

1. Zoom out on your life

The challenge with our feelings is that it's hard to detect patterns while we're in the midst of them. It's why others can spot our emotional trends but we can't. We're often too deep in the daily emotions to see the broader context.

So, it is necessary to take a step back in order to evaluate your life. Pretend to be an impartial observer studying your life as data, seeking proof. Your past experiences can be treated as valuable data for making deductions. We go through numerous emotions and actions each day, majority of them recurrent.

Ask yourself:

What negative emotions repeat themselves in your life?

What negative behaviors repeat themselves in your life?

---

2. Work to discover your emotional triggers

Our behaviors can show up in various forms, but they generally stem from similar deep seated feelings. Even if you can't pinpoint the feelings immediately, you can typically figure out what prompts your emotions. These prompts act as hints to discern your actual emotions.

For instance, I often become excessively judgmental when feeling exposed or weak. This habit resulted in numerous disagreements with my significant other during the early years of our relationship. I was unclear about the root of my anger. Rather than seeking the source, I merely showed my feelings via my behavior.

However, when I started to analyze triggers for my anger, I saw reality. Instances of vulnerability led to my critical attitude. Now, if I feel overly critical, I investigate potential causes of my vulnerability.

Ask yourself:

What causes a change in your emotions or behaviors?

What different situations often prompt the same behavioral response?

---

3. Interrupt the pattern and address the emotion

Grasping your feelings and what sparks them doesn't imply they'll cease straight away. Keep in mind, your brain and habits have been shaped over many years. However, knowing yourself better will aid in breaking the harmful cycle and dealing directly with the emotion itself.

Recognizing your emotional trends is the first step. Spot when these patterns start. Don't let them control you stop them. Realize they're not helpful. Then, take time to dig deeper into your actual emotions.

From there, you can discover what you need.

Ask yourself:

What clues can you use to recognize when you're engaging in a negative emotional pattern?

How can you interrupt the negative pattern and replace it with a healthier alternative?

How can you design your environment in a way to reinforce more positive patterns?

9. THE POWER OF SHADOW WORK JOURNALING

Writing about feelings is a strong method for gaining clear thoughts, understanding oneself, and seeing different viewpoints. When you use writing as a way to really feel and deeply examine your emotions without criticizing, you invite important lessons that encourage individual progress and learning.

Writing in a diary to understand feelings can allow you to recognize and sort out your emotions. It also allows you to discover their root cause and figure out the most effective way to react to them. Writing about your feelings can assist in clearly identifying them. With continued effort, you'll be able to point out "I am angry" or "I am scared." Knowing your emotions allows you to handle them effectively.

As you put in the effort to jot down in a diary, you're not just letting emotions flow freely but also gaining better scene understanding. The moment you empty out those overwhelming sentiments in a diary, you can revisit your previously penned lines to understand better your deeds and the way you reacted.

Why Journaling Works

Shadow work journaling originates from Jung's concept of lighting up the unconscious. It urges you to explore the "shadowy" aspects of your persona, allowing healing and understanding instead of denial or suppression. Shadow work takes an additional leap, indicating that these hidden features can hold keys to motivation and enlightenment.

A shadow diary is a spot to note and sort through the trickier or unsettling aspects of your character impartially. The act of such diary writing is commonly termed "inner exploration" because it needs an individual to bravely be truthful to themselves.

Essentially, shadow work is about examining the aspects of yourself that you're not fond of. Then, accepting them as parts that require care and focus.

Think of someone wrestling with fierce envy. Such potent jealousy hinders their progress. They're too busy comparing themselves to others than concentrating on personal ambitions. When a buddy shares a success story, they can seem joyous. But they grapple with inner anger, perhaps secretly hoping others stumble. This person becomes painfully aware of their jealousy, recoiling in shame. They strive to stifle these emotions, but the suppression seemingly magnifies these undesirable feelings.

Writing in a shadow journal can allow a person to uncover the source of their feelings. This knowledge will let them grasp their own desires more deeply. They can turn this comprehension into personal triumph, while also becoming the reliably encouraging individual they long to be.

Grasping the way journaling about your shadow enhances self-improvement requires initial acknowledgment of your shadow's influence on your well-being. You could begin by comparing your shadow traits to "acting out kids" who are brushed aside, held accountable for all mishaps, and repeatedly admonished for misbehavior.

Think about a kid who only hears words of blame and regret. Hiding and feeling guilty about the less pleasant sides of your character can result in:

- Anxiety
- Depression
- Self sabotage
- Self-loathing
- Poor self-esteem
- Offensive or even violent behavior toward others
- Unhealthy and unsatisfying relationships
- Being self-absorbed and egotistical
- Dishonesty with yourself and others
- Thoughts of self-harm or suicide

Folks who deny their darker sides often transfer bad feelings to others. This is called projecting, where you get bothered by others showing the same failings you know but overlook in yourself. Rather than shutting them out, shadow work welcomes these "naughty kids" into a caring environment. Here, they can feel loved, guided, and appreciated without any condition.

A journal for shadow work is a safe space. You can record and think about the negative or troubling parts of your character without fear of criticism. Often called "searching your soul," this exercise requires genuine honesty. A shadow work journal is for recording and thinking about the not so nice parts of one's personality. You do it without fear of being judged. Shadow work digs into a person's soul, pushing people to face and accept their less attractive sides. This deep look is to show them love and care.

Imagine a person feeling envy and jealousy, something that could potentially spoil their success. They always compare themselves to others, not focusing on their own dreams. Outwardly they seem happy when a friend shares good news. But inside they feel anger and secretly wish for others' failure. In such a situation, the person realizes their envy and feels embarrassed. They try to hide these feelings. Yet the more they do, they get bigger and harder to control.

People can use shadow work journaling methods to dive deep into their feelings. It leads to a great personal insight and helps understand the reasons behind their actions. With this fresh perspective, they can promote their success and change into the uplifting person they desire to be.

Those who refuse to accept their own flaws often project their negative thoughts onto others. Projection occurs when one becomes upset with others who display negative qualities that they themselves possess but choose to overlook.

Instead of suppressing them, shadow work invites these "misbehaving children" into a nurturing environment where they can be embraced, guided, and loved without conditions.

So here are some of the many perks that come with shadow journaling:

INCREASED SELF-AWARENESS

When a car malfunctions, one doesn't simply park the vehicle in the garage and label it as a "bad car" that doesn't work. Instead, it is taken to a knowledgeable mechanic who can repair it and address the issue properly. The concept of shadow work operates in pretty much the same way.

In this way, the utilization of shadow journaling can help in heightening self-awareness. The deeper you understand your inner workings, the more adept you become at tending to your own well-being.

CLARITY

In uncomfortable situations, people often find themselves trapped in repetitive emotional patterns that can result in impulsive reactions. To address this, shadow work encourages individuals to delve deeper into their emotions and examine their responses.

When you are willing to introspect, even during moments of anger or shame, you can gain a much better understanding of your behavior. Rather than pushing down emotions such as envy, people engaging in shadow work may reflect, "Ah, that feeling again. I wonder why I'm reacting this way when what I really want to do is offer support."

A MORE FULFILLING EXISTENCE

Jung argued that the integration of one's shadow qualities has the potential to enhance life fulfillment. Getting into shadow work allows people to address the underlying causes of their mental struggles. By acknowledging, embracing, and assimilating the aspects of ourselves that we tend to overlook, suppress, or deny, we can gain a much better understanding of our true essence and cultivate a more balanced sense of self.

RELATIONSHIP HEALING

When we feel the need to hide a part of our personality or project our negative traits onto others, it becomes nearly impossible to build a healthy relationship. Engaging in shadow work can effectively reduce projection. This, then, enables us to interact with others in a more genuine manner, leading to an increased sense of compassion for both ourselves and those around us. Through this process, we come to recognize ourselves as complete individuals, facing internal battles that need to be overcome. As a result, forgiving and understanding others becomes a far easier task. All of this leads to healthier and healed relationships.

EMOTIONAL RESILIENCE

Exploring one's shadow side can bring up some unpleasant stuff too. It may stir up negative emotions and painful memories. However, confronting these difficult aspects can actually be good for us. Often, individuals shy away from delving into their darker side out of fear that the discomfort or embarrassment that comes with it will overwhelm them.

Engaging in challenging tasks can actually enhance your emotional resilience. The more you are willing to confront your inner struggles, the greater your capacity for personal growth and accomplishment becomes.

HONESTY AND VULNERABILITY

One must question how honesty with others can be achieved if there is a lack of honesty with oneself. By being unwilling to open up and show vulnerability, how can you expect others to trust you enough to reciprocate this vulnerability? A useful tool in addressing both of these issues is the practice of maintaining a shadow work journal.

As one embraces honesty and explores their own emotions, they gain the ability to extend these practices to people that are important to them in their life's journey.

Getting Started With Shadow Work Journaling

As mentioned above, engaging in shadow work has the potential to facilitate personal growth and revive forgotten talents and aspirations. However, embarking on this journey requires a firm commitment. It is important to be prepared for the possibility that some of your deeply held beliefs might be challenged.

When one becomes more skilled at keeping a journal, it is important to remember that the goal is to observe oneself rather than pass judgment on one's behavior or choices.

FIND SUPPORT

Writing about your shadow traits can be an emotionally triggering experience, so it may be wise to get a support system in place before you start a shadow journal. Working with a mental health professional isn't required, but it may be the best approach if you have mental health concerns. Otherwise, joining a support group or speaking with a trusted friend about your plans to do shadow journaling may provide the support you need if the process gets difficult.

DISCOVERING YOUR ELUSIVE SHADOW

Each individual carries their own inner demons, their shadow self, which accompanies them throughout their daily existence. However, it requires practice and self-awareness to identify these shadow behaviors. These behaviors emerge as a result of underlying emotions and are manifested through our actions.

There are many instances of shadow behaviors that can surface:

- Engaging in the dissemination of malicious rumors within the workplace.
- Defensive behavior.
- Extreme jealousy.
- Engaging in the deliberate sabotage of others.
- In the midst of heated arguments, engaging in name calling or intentionally inflicting emotional harm upon your partner may occur.
- Self sabotaging actions such as excessive spending.
- When faced with any inconvenience, responding with an exaggerated display of anger, sarcasm, or even rage.

In many instances, it is often easier to recognize shadow traits in others rather than acknowledging them within oneself. However, one can harness the power of projection to their advantage. If faced with difficulty in identifying one's own shadow traits, it may be helpful to reflect on something that bothers you about another person. It is highly likely that the negativity observed in others is a reflection and projection of one's own shadow.

THE IMPORTANCE OF ESTABLISHING A CLEAR OBJECTIVE TO PURSUE

Engaging in shadow work journaling serves a purpose and should be an ongoing practice. Setting a goal at the beginning of your shadow work journey can be beneficial. However, it is important to acknowledge that as you delve deeper into self-reflection, your goals may evolve. In fact, genuine personal growth often entails a shift in objectives.

Consider the objectives you aim to achieve by maintaining a journal for shadow work. Are you seeking to enhance personal relationships or attain professional ambitions? Perhaps you yearn to break free from the hold of negative emotions and behaviors so that you can progress and develop. It is essential to acknowledge that there is no definitive right or wrong reason to embark on shadow work. Your motivations are valid, irrespective of their nature.

When journaling, it is important to set realistic goals. Instead of viewing your efforts as pass or fail, understand that progress can be made even without amazing insights. It's perfectly fine if you spend an hour writing in your journal and don't uncover any profound revelations. Sometimes, the most valuable insights come when you least expect them.

If one's schedule or energy permits, writing in a journal once a week is sufficient. It is important to acknowledge that shadow work can be emotionally draining and thus it isessential to proceed at one's own pace and find a method that works best for them.

Allow yourself to be guided by the journey ahead. The process of personal growth is often a mix of gradual progress and sudden breakthroughs. It is essential to let go of expectations, both for yourself and your endeavors.

UNEARTHING YOUR INNER DEMONS

Let's say you have identified certain aspects of your personality that you consider to be shadow traits. You have sought support and have started journaling. Yet, the question remains: What exactly does it entail to engage in shadow work? The process of delving into one's shadow can be as straightforward as analyzing one's behavioral patterns in response to triggers.

For example, someone might feel slighted when a fellow colleague receives more recognition for a group task than is perceived as deserved. This individual then documents the incident in their shadow work journal, discovering a recurring feeling of being overlooked. Interestingly, they also possess a tendency to attribute credit for their own work to others.

Now that you see the situation more clearly, you can behave differently. Instead of being angry at someone else for excelling, you can become a better self-advocate, take more leadership roles, and allow others to see your efforts.

BONUS PAGES

By purchasing this book, you gain access to exclusive bonus content designed to complement your journey through the "Authentic Shadow Work Workbook & Journal For Beginners." This special gift includes guided meditations, visualizations, daily affirmations, and more, all crafted to deepen your understanding and enhance your practice of shadow work. To access your free content, simply scan the QR code at the bottom of this page with your smartphone's camera, and follow the link that appears.

QR

Enjoy this thoughtful addition to your self-discovery journey!

Tips And Techniques For Using A Shadow Journal

To make the most of your shadow journaling experience, simply follow these steps.

1. When engaging in shadow work journaling, it is not necessary to isolate oneself completely. However, it is important to keep in mind that this practice can elicit deep emotions. It is advisable to choose a comfortable and secure space where you can freely express and explore your emotions through writing.

2. There are days when one may approach journaling with a clear idea or topic in mind. Whereas, on other occasions, the specific subject to document may be uncertain. If someone is unsure about what to write, a writing prompt can be a helpful tool. The Day One journaling app offers a wide range of prompts that can enhance your journaling experience, regardless of the topic you choose.

3. When individuals embark on their journaling journey, they may encounter the initial challenge of filling a page with words. It might be necessary to push oneself to write for a designated duration of time. Conversely, one can become so engrossed in journal writing that they lose all sense of time. In either scenario, employing a timer proves to be an effective solution.

4. The journal belongs to the individual, granting them the freedom to utilize it according to their preferences. There are no set guidelines that restrict the inclusion of text only when engaging in shadow work journaling. Feel free to incorporate drawing, photos, collages, symbols, or even emojis. Express yourself in whichever manner feels most genuine and appropriate in the moment. Remember that the work of the unconscious is often expressed in metaphors. Your doodle may trigger something in your memory that a well-crafted, double spaced, spellchecked page of text never would.

5. Engaging in self-reflection forms the core of meaningful shadow work. An integral part of this process involves not only creating new journal entries but also revisiting previous ones. As you peruse the pages of your journal, pay attention to recurring patterns in your thoughts and behaviors. These patterns might offer valuable insights into your shadow traits.

When individuals gain more experience in shadow work journaling, they inevitably develop their own unique system and style. However, it is vital to have a sense of confidence in the process before this personalization can occur. To enhance the meaningfulness of your journaling practice, here are some valuable tips to consider:

- The experience of both joy and pain should be written down.
- In the face of challenges, it is important to maintain honesty with oneself.
- Embrace every instance of progress, no matter how small it may seem.
- Write about every step of the self-discovery journey.
- View your progress with an impartial gaze instead of judging yourself with a biased perspective.
- Grasp the importance of embracing uncomfortable truths.
- Acknowledge the fact that you are making an effort to achieve your goals.

Shadow work aftercare should not be overlooked. It is important to establish routines that aid in restoring emotional balance when engaging in journaling brings up distressing memories or emotions. These routines can prove to be beneficial in managing and coping with such situations.

It can be beneficial to conclude each writing session with a positive affirmation, such as "I fully embrace myself," "I am forgiving of my mistakes," or "I take pride in my personal growth." This practice has the potential to be advantageous for individuals engaged in the writing process.

It may also be beneficial to arrange a coffee meetup with a companion or engage in self-care activities following an emotionally intense journaling session. For instance, taking a stroll or preparing a nutritious meal can help recharge your energy after focusing on personal growth. This recharging process promotes both motivation and fulfillment, preparing you for your next journaling session.

As you get better at shadow work journaling, you'll create your own methods and flair. Until you're sure of this process, these suggestions can help make your journaling more significant:

- Describe your joy and pain
- Be honest with yourself, even when it's difficult
- Celebrate all growth, even if it's a small step
- Enjoy the journey of learning about yourself
- Observe without judgment
- Understand the need for uncomfortable truths
- Celebrate the fact that you are trying

Remember that aftercare for shadow work is important. Creating habits that help level out and fix your emotions can assist when writing sparks troubling memories or feelings.

Emotional Journaling Techniques

There are various kinds of emotional diary methods that can assist you in better connecting with your feelings. Every tactic offers distinct advantages. Trying diverse kinds of creative writing could be a great way to make your diary writing livelier and more successful.

STREAM OF CONSCIOUSNESS WRITING

Writing as thoughts come to mind is one special kind of writing. It's like capturing every thought, feeling, and sensation in a pure, unaltered way, just as they pop up in your mind. This kind of diary practice encourages being spontaneous, and can unveil hidden feelings and understanding.

When you're stuck with what to pen down, jot silly words, hummable tunes, or whatever pops in your head. Keep the pen moving, and before you know it, ideas will start to form again.

REFLECTIVE JOURNALING

Pause for a bit and think about your day or a particular happening. Jot down what you were thinking, how you felt, and what you saw. Using the method of a pondering diary promotes understanding of self and helps you comprehend your feelings better.

PROMPT-BASED JOURNALING

Writing prompts serve as questions, ideas, or assertions that spur introspection. These are particularly valuable on occasions when your feelings are mixed up and starting from scratch seems daunting. They can occasionally evoke unforeseen emotions. Even a basic inquiry might direct you toward profound understanding of how you voice and manage your emotions.

DIALOGUE JOURNALING

Chat with your feelings, ideas, or a certain person or character through writing. Note down their replies as if it were a real talk. This method lets you explore and understand your inner world better.

CREATIVE WRITING

Writing in a diary usually relates to real life, yet spicing it up with some creative storytelling methods can be interesting and helpful. Turning a difficult memory from history into something fictional might make it easier to pen down. Incorporating creative aspects might also assist you in recognizing the feelings of the leading character and bring out strong internal realizations about your own emotions.

LETTER WRITING

Write a letter to yourself, a person, or an idea. Share your feelings, wants, and issues. This method gives relief and can lead to understanding and closure.

MINDFULNESS JOURNALING

Join together personal writing and present moment awareness. Stopping for a moment before beginning your writing to completely experience your emotions without opinion can benefit you. It helps to fully grasp your feelings and thoughts. This combination of stopping and then writing assists in accepting yourself and understanding your emotions.

FUTURE JOURNALING

Picture the future you dream of, or a target you'd like to hit. Jot it down, noting the feelings and events involved with that objective. This strategy aids you in seeing your goals more clearly and making your actions match your hoped for results.

GRATITUDE JOURNALING

Keeping a gratitude journal is a favored way to boost good vibes. There are many tactics to apply this idea: perhaps penning down minimum three good things at the close of each day. Writing extensively on a single thankfulness theme is another strategy. Owning a gratitude journal comes with a myriad of advantages for your mental and physical well-being.

TRACK EMOTIONAL PATTERNS AND TRIGGERS

Track small details like the following and look for trends:

- The weather that day
- What you ate
- What was on your mind before your journaling session
- How you felt when you woke up that morning
- Whether you were experiencing distress or conflict
- Whether you had a restful sleep the night before

Remember your feelings as best as you can, like you're jotting down facts. No need to make judgments or criticisms. Write about your emotions as if observing someone else. When you look back at your journal entries, trends might start to appear. Maybe you realize you're upset when you leave specific places or get irritable whenever it rains. Tiny things can sometimes matter a lot. They could help better your life.

ACTIVITY 8:
Journal Prompts for Emotional Journaling

Use these prompts in your journal.

What emotion am I feeling right now?

....
....
....

Where do I feel this emotion in my body?

....
....
....

What physical feelings do I notice when I have this emotion? Does it show up in a certain area of my body or in a unique manner?

....
....
....

What triggered this emotion?

....
....
....

How am I responding to this emotion?

When was the last time I felt this way?

What emotions do I feel most often?

What emotions do I avoid feeling?

How did my emotions affect my thoughts and behavior today?

What can I learn from this emotion?

....
....
....

How can I express this emotion in a healthy way?

....
....
....

What were some moments of stress or frustration today?

....
....
....

What were some moments of peace or calm today?

....
....
....

How can I support myself through this emotion?

....
....
....

What feelings of guilt or shame have I experienced lately?

What are the underlying beliefs or fears that might be driving my feelings of guilt or shame, and how can I address them in a constructive way?

How do I think others perceive me? How does this perception differ from how I perceive myself, and what might this reveal about my shadow aspects?

What have others communicated to me about myself? How have these comments affected my self-image, and what do they reveal about qualities I may not be fully aware of?

When was the last time I reacted to a situation strongly or defensively? What might this reaction reveal about an unresolved issue or hidden aspect within myself?

How do I respond to compliments? What emotions or beliefs might be influencing my reactions to praise, and how can I work on embracing my positive qualities?

....
....
....

What is a recurring pattern in my relationships or life circumstances? What might this pattern say about my unconscious beliefs or fears?

....
....
....

What is a trait or behavior in others that triggers annoyance or discomfort in me? How might this be a reflection of something within myself that I need to address?

....
....
....

When do I feel valued and loved? Are there times when I struggle to accept love or feel undeserving? What might this say about my relationship with myself?

....
....
....

What challenges did I face as a child? How have these challenges shaped my adult self, and what unresolved issues might still be affecting me today?

What are my best and worst traits? How can I identify any patterns or connections between these traits, and how can I work to integrate and balance them?

What is a part about myself that I feel shame, guilt, or embarrassment about? How can I offer understanding, compassion, and acceptance to myself?

Think about a time when you felt out of control or overwhelmed by your emotions. What can this experience teach you about your unmet needs or unexpressed feelings?

What do I need to forgive myself for?

How has holding onto guilt or regret impacted my life, and what steps can I take toward self-forgiveness and healing?

What do I judge others for, and why? How might these judgments reflect my own insecurities or unacknowledged qualities?

Reflect on a past decision or action that you regret. How can you reframe this experience as an opportunity for growth and self-forgiveness?

Write a dialogue between your inner critic and your inner nurturer. What would each voice say to the other, and how can they find common ground?

How do I support others? Do I show myself that same love?

What do I consider to be healthy boundaries? Are there areas in my life where I struggle to set or maintain boundaries, and what might this reveal about my needs or fears?

What are some limiting beliefs you hold about yourself or your abilities? Where do these beliefs come from, and how can you challenge them?

When do I feel the need to lie? What is the worst lie I've told?

What motivates me to be dishonest, and how might this relate to my shadow aspects?

What parts of myself do I hide? Why do I feel the need to conceal these aspects, and how can I work on accepting and integrating them into my whole self?

When do I feel most authentic and true to myself? In which situations or relationships do I find it challenging to be my authentic self, and what might this reveal about my hidden fears or beliefs?

．．

．．

．．

What are some dreams, aspirations, or desires that I have suppressed or abandoned? How do these unfulfilled dreams relate to my shadow aspects, and what can I do to rekindle or honor these parts of myself?

．．

．．

．．

If I imagine I am at the end of my life, looking back on the journey I've taken, what advice or guidance would I offer to my younger self about embracing and integrating my shadow aspects?

．．

．．

．．

Remember that shadow work can be an intense and emotional process, so be gentle with yourself as you explore these prompts. If you find that any prompt brings up strong emotions or feels too overwhelming, consider seeking support from a mental health professional or a trusted friend.

10. THE MYSTERY OF ARCHETYPES:
UNVEILING INVISIBLE FORCES

Carl Jung believed that archetypes are "timeless types, holding universal pictures that have been around since the ancient times." These exist in the Collective Unconscious. Archetypes are not learned, they are instinctive and shared by everyone, passed down through generations and help shape our understanding and experience of the world.

Carl Jung disagreed with the idea that our minds are empty at birth and only shaped by life events. Instead, he felt that our minds hold marks from our ancestors handed down to us. These are unseen, "ancient pictures," or archetypes. We can find archetypes even in the earliest tales and myths of mankind.

The Essence Of Archetypes

Carl Jung had a theory that our brains have three parts: the Ego, the Personal Unconscious, and the Collective Unconscious. Jung explained that the Ego stands for the aware mind. The Personal Unconscious shows the learned or gotten experiences. Lastly, the Collective Unconscious is a part that everyone shares.

Jung explains the Collective Unconscious as a "shared, universal, and impartial system that stays the same in everyone. This shared unconscious isn't something we grow into, but something we're born with. It's made up of preexisting models, the archetypes, that only later become known. These models shape specific mental states" (*The Archetypes and the Collective Unconscious*, 1959).

THE MOTHER ARCHETYPE

Carl Jung refers to the Mother Archetype. He says it is often linked to symbols of fertility and abundance, like the horn of plenty, tilled land, and gardens. This Archetype can be connected to solid objects like rocks, caves, trees, springs, deep wells, or even vessels shaped like flowers, such as roses or lotuses. Furthermore, Jung also discusses how the Mother Archetype appears in things like ovens and cooking pots, and naturally, forms like the uterus and yoni. This Archetype may also be visible in intimidating symbols like a witch, dragons, or large engulfing animals like big fish or snakes, graves, caskets, deep waters, death, and eerie dreams.

The Mother Archetype embodies traits like caring, understanding, knowledge, supportive actions or feelings, everything that's kind, everything that nurtures and supports, that encourages growth and strength. However, dark aspects of the Mother Archetype might include everything that's hidden, shadowy, deep, a frightening underworld, all things that consume, tempt, and harm or that are scary and can't be escaped, like destiny.

THE CHILD ARCHETYPE

The Child Archetype is often depicted by earth bound animals like crocodiles, dragons, snakes, or monkeys. Sometimes, the archetype is shown in a flower or emerging from a golden egg. It could also be the main point of a circular design. In dreams, it may show up as the dreamer's child or as a young person; sometimes it could seem to come from a foreign place like India or China. It might even appear surrounded by stars or wearing a crown of stars.

Jung explains the Child Archetype in simple terms. It can appear as a king's son or a witch's child with supernatural traits. It can also be viewed as a special form of the "hard to get treasure" idea. The child idea takes many forms. It can look like a jewel, pearl, flower, gold egg, or even a golden ball. These symbols can freely replace the child. In folk tales, the child idea shows up as a dwarf or an elf. These represent unseen natural forces. Jung also points out that the Child Archetype can show up as a "sudden unconscious surge." European ghost stories serve as an example of this.

THE TRICKSTER ARCHETYPE

Jung describes the Trickster Archetype as someone who enjoys crafty jokes and harmful tricks, has the ability to change their form, has a twin like persona, half beast, half god, faces all types of punishments, and is also a bit like a hero. In an added explanation, Jung claims that the Trickster Archetype, despite being an entirely negative hero, can accomplish through his foolishness what others cannot manage even with their most ardent attempts.

Carl Jung discusses how the Trickster Archetype shows a mindset that's more beast like, unlike anything sacred. In Jung's perspective, the Trickster Archetype is clearly a "psychlogem," an ancient symbolic mental construct. He suggests that it mirrors a completely uniform human consciousness, similar to a mindset that is barely above that of an animal.

THE SHADOW ARCHETYPE

The Shadow Archetype stands for a part of our subconscious that we keep masked, a part that our ego declines. It holds raw impulses like the desire to reproduce, to continue living, or viewed biblically, the "sinful human nature." For instance, it is human nature for us to feel certain emotions that may not be socially acceptable, such as hate, envy, disrespect, or lust. These emotions could lead to harmful situations if expressed openly. If these feelings weren't suppressed, they could result in problems that could badly impact our social standings.

THE PERSONA ARCHETYPE

The Persona is our self-representation when others are watching. The term "persona" comes from a Greek word meaning "mask." Instead of a physical mask, the persona works like a mental mask. We wear it to show a specific image.

Jung suggests, the persona can shift in various social environments, serving as a protector for the ego so it isn't seen in a poor light. The persona can also act as safeguard, preventing the Shadow from cropping up in unfitting situations. From this standpoint, it's clear that the growing teenager recognizes that society has its own rules and standards. Hence, the child must employ their persona to manage all the basic urges, feelings and instincts that society might not approve of. People showing strong signs of the Persona Archetype, like over connecting with their public image, demonstrate what we call a "Neurosis."

Understanding Carl Jung Archetypes can be a bit tough but also very intriguing. Once you get the basic idea, you might start noticing Archetypes in a lot of new movies or books, and possibly in yourself as well.

ENCOUNTERING YOUR ARCHETYPES

Discovering your key types is an essential part of shadow work. It uncovers signs of usual patterns and core parts of the human mind. Key types, as defined by Carl Jung, are basic symbols and themes that we all inherit. They live inside our unconscious mind.

In shadow exploration, people might meet archetypes. These are like different parts of their mind taking form. They can show up as different characters, symbols, or ideas in dreams, daydreams, or thoughtful reflections. Each archetype has its own feel and sign. They often echo a person's personality, wants, worries, or traits they might not see in themselves.

Meeting familiar figures opens the door to better understanding ourselves. Say you come across the "wise sage" character. This might mean you need to listen to your gut more or seek advice before deciding on something. On the flip side, if you run into the "shadow" character, it could symbolize that you should examine things about yourself that you've pushed aside or ignored.

So, interacting with well-known roles lets people search their character and grasp the mix of bright and darker elements inside them. By identifying and absorbing these common energy forms, a person can get a balanced, calm inner self.

Experiencing common patterns in shadow work often results in deep realizations and personal changes. Interacting with these symbolic signs helps folks explore their own minds more, letting them understand their own actions, habits, and chances to improve better.

In the end, finding typical models in the realm of shadow work gives you a path to know yourself better. It provides deep understanding of the many sides of the human mind. It encourages people to accept and tie together these symbolic images. This promotes personal development, self-knowledge, and a stronger link to the hidden powers that form their lives.

ARCHETYPES AND THE COLLECTIVE UNCONSCIOUS

Jung agreed that the concept of a "collective unconscious" seems odd but eventually becomes a familiar notion to people. It was a concept he had to protect from claims of mysticism. He pointed out that people once dismissed the idea of an unconscious mind as a whim, until Freud showed it existed. Then, it became central to our understanding of human behavior and thought. Freud viewed the unconscious as a personal thing, existing within a person: "The preconscious contains thoughts and feelings that a person is not currently aware of, but which can easily be brought to consciousness" (A General Introduction to Psychoanalysis, 1924). Jung, conversely, believed that this deeper layer he called the "collective unconscious" was the inherited part of our psyche, not shaped by personal experiences.

Collective subconscious is communicated via archetypes, or common mental patterns that sway a person's feelings and actions. These archetypes don't usually care much for societal norms, implying they are inherent. A newborn isn't an empty canvas. Instead, they are set up to recognize specific archetypal designs. That's why kids have such great imaginations as, according to Jung, they haven't faced enough real world encounters to override their brain's enjoyment of these primal images.

Archetypes are often seen in myths and bedtime stories, and even in our dreams and thoughts. In the study of mythology, they're known as "motifs." The field of anthropology dubs them "collective representations." Adolf Bastian, a German ethnologist, called them "elementary" or "ancient" ideas. He found these ideas kept surfacing in the traditions of different tribes and folks. But, they're not only fascinating from an anthropological perspective; these archetypes also subtly influence the relationships that are important to us, even when we're unaware of it.

Archetypes And Complexes

Why is the study of the mind fairly recent? Jung posited that its formulation was not needed for a good part of history. The rich symbols and stories embedded in faiths were just fine expressing profound eternal concepts. People often mull over notions and pictures about renewal and evolution, which are found abundantly in religious beliefs to cater to every mental need. Intriguing concepts like the Virgin Birth and the Trinity in Catholicism are not mere imaginary figures. Instead, according to Jung, they are filled with deep significance. These notions of safety and recovery tended to emotional wounds among believers.

The Protestant Reformation countered everything before it. What was once vibrant Catholic symbolism and doctrine, turned into mere "superstition." Jung believed this shift paved the way for today's modern life void of depth. Authentic spirituality calls for the interaction of both our unconscious and conscious thoughts, diving deep as well as rising high.

Jung noticed that Westerners were drawn to Eastern religions, although he believed it wasn't needed due to the rich symbolism found in Christianity. He also saw individuals being drawn toward political and social concepts known for their lack of spiritual joy. People possess a spiritual instinct, suggests Jung, whether that's faith in God or a belief in societal structures such as communism or atheism. He noted that being human involves unavoidable bias.

INDIVIDUATION

"Individuation" is a term coined by Jung. It signifies the moment when a person manages to combine their inner contrasts their conscious and unconscious thoughts. Individuation is about realizing your inherent potential to achieve your unique promise. The end result? An actual individual, a complete and unbreakable self that is immune to the influence of fragmented aspects or complexes.

Re-piecing our lives isn't just about focused thinking. It's a trip full of surprising bends and curves. Tons of legends illustrate that we must take a journey beyond logic to find happiness in life. Jung really explored the idea of the self. He defined it as different from the ego, thinking of it like a big circle that includes a smaller one. The ego ties to our active thoughts, while the self is a part of unseen, personal and shared feelings.

THE HEALING MANDALA

Jung's work, *Archetypes and the Collective Unconscious*, contains numerous mandala images—abstract designs, named in Sanskrit for "circle." He theorized that creating a mandala allows a person's hidden desires or tendencies to emerge through its patterns, symbols, and forms.

Jung, in his therapy work, saw mandalas have a "magical" impact. They turned chaos into order, influenced people in ways that weren't clear at first. This happened because the unconscious mind was let loose, revealing hidden things. Symbols like egg shapes, a snake, a star, or a city were drawn without any apparent reason. However, they were pulling out processes happening deeply beneath someone's conscious thought. When a person began to understand these images, Jung noticed it usually marked the start of mental healing. It was a step in the journey of individuation.

We believe ourselves to be advanced and cultured due to our vast technology and wisdom, but according to Jung, our inner selves are still "ancient." He witnessed a phenomenon in Switzerland where a Strudel, a traditional healer, lifted a curse from a barn while fast trans-European trains passed by in the background.

Navigating The Archetypal Landscape

Exploring the common landscape in shadow work involves a journey of self-examination, understanding, and combination. Here's a guide to move around this complex territory.

Building knowledge means tuning into the minor details of universal symbols, roles, or topics that appear in different ways—dreams, daily life, or artistic creations. This fine tuning helps people spot patterns, recurrences, or strong feelings connected to these symbols. It's about fostering an increased awareness of things that awaken interest, connection, or unease within one's own mind.

Acknowledge the existence and importance of stuff you run into all the time, like the "old wise guy," the "joker," or themes like the "hero's voyage." You see that they're there and you start to realize that they mean more. This means understanding these symbols or people apply to you. They show you parts of yourself you haven't seen or knew were there.

Understanding these models is a journey of consciousness. This phase requires self-reflection to figure out their symbolic meanings and the lessons they bring. It's about thinking deeply about these models—how they echo within us, our wants, or unrecognized parts of ourselves. Diving into their symbolic values and discovering how they impact us personally, we learn about their importance related to our feelings, character qualities, or life situations.

Also, considering and mulling over cultivates a deeper comprehension of archetypes' importance in our life's journey. It probes their links to earlier happenings, relationships, or existing hurdles. Pondering over the messages of archetypes, people start a journey of learning more about themselves. They slowly uncover layers of their subconscious, gaining useful understanding into their internal functions. They also realize the change that these meetings could spark within them.

Exploring and conversing involves actively interacting with the encountered symbols. This step includes using activities like daydreaming, relaxing, or writing to build a stronger connection and grasp of their meanings. Through these activities, people make a welcoming environment for conversation, allowing these symbols to share their knowledge, details, and unseen parts. Talking with these symbolic figures lets people ask deep questions, seek advice, and find out how these symbols apply to their current lives. This deep diving exploration fosters an intense understanding of the symbols' messages, promoting a stronger bond with these parts of the mind.

Joining together and changing are the next steps in the process. It's about accepting the combination of unique energies, taking on board the lessons, strengths, or ideas shown through these symbols. The task is to take in this knowledge, use it in everyday life. This joining process is about understanding and meshing together the different sides of the symbols within ourselves—making peace between good and bad, accepting positive qualities and weaknesses. By acknowledging these different energies, people can grow personally, find inner peace, and self-understanding in a well-rounded way.

Indeed, joining elements is not just about intellectually grasping these templates; it's about living their core and using their knowledge to tackle life's difficulties. This method helps in synchronizing actions, notions, and feelings with the acquired understanding, cultivating a congruent and genuine feel in one's life.

Looking for help means understanding complex situations and the value of getting help from seasoned authorities. Pros like therapists, counselors, or guides who know about deep psychology or shadow work can provide great advice. Their deep knowledge gives a strong foundation for handling these hard aspects of the mind. Through their help, people can uncover more about themselves, gain tools for self-thought, and learn how to handle tough situations. This outside view can reveal hidden elements, provide assurance and deepen self-discovery, fostering a deeper personal journey.

The idea of Continued Exploration says our journey never stops. This means our search within ourselves is always changing. Being curious and open minded is at the heart of this constant hunt. The realm we are exploring is massive and always changing, giving us limitless chances to understand ourselves better. This unending journey helps us welcome new knowledge, dig deeper into uncharted areas, and grow within our ever shifting mindset. It invites a promise to never stop learning about ourselves, nurturing a curiosity and wonder as we journey through our complex inner world.

Exploring the classic scenery with interest, self-examining, and a ready spirit for self-discovery helps people gain deep knowledge. This helps them change personally, and build a better understanding of their complex and symbolic mind traits.

ACTIVITY 9:
Self-Archetype Quiz

Answer the following questions and keep score, which you will calculate at the end to find out which archetype you most relate to. There are four of these archetypes that you can access.

Read each question and rate yourself on a scale of 0–5 for each.

0 = Never   2 = On occasion   4 = Often
1 = Hardly ever   3 = Sometimes   5 = Most of the time

PART A

0 1 2 3 4 5

1. I need to create a world I feel strong in.
2. I need to feel in control.
3. People tell me I am a good leader.
4. I can be called bossy.
5. I like movies about Kings and Queens.
6. I enjoy the challenge of bringing order to messy situations.

ADD UP YOUR TOTAL FOR PART A ➡

PART B

0 1 2 3 4 5

1. I love learning almost anything.
2. People often ask for my advice.
3. Having a library is important to me.
4. I enjoy movies that honor wisdom.
5. Sometimes, I can get lost in a dream world of ideas.
6. I am considered a pretty serious person.

ADD UP YOUR TOTAL FOR PART B ➡

PART C

	0	1	2	3	4	5
1. The greatest joy for me is to make good things happen.	☐	☐	☐	☐	☐	☐
2. I enjoy films about the occult or magic.	☐	☐	☐	☐	☐	☐
3. Mystery intrigues me.	☐	☐	☐	☐	☐	☐
4. People count on me to change things.	☐	☐	☐	☐	☐	☐
5. Some say I have a healing effect on them.	☐	☐	☐	☐	☐	☐
6. It's important to know what you want in life.	☐	☐	☐	☐	☐	☐

ADD UP YOUR TOTAL FOR PART C ➡ ☐

PART D

	0	1	2	3	4	5
1. I can easily make others laugh.	☐	☐	☐	☐	☐	☐
2. I can be a bit sneaky if I have to be.	☐	☐	☐	☐	☐	☐
3. I like to tell the truth in a non-serious way.	☐	☐	☐	☐	☐	☐
4. When things go really wrong, you just have to laugh at the silliness of it all.	☐	☐	☐	☐	☐	☐
5. I like to watch comedy on TV and in the movies.	☐	☐	☐	☐	☐	☐
6. Life should be enjoyed.	☐	☐	☐	☐	☐	☐

ADD UP YOUR TOTAL FOR PART D ➡ ☐

Now look at your total for each part A through D.

- If you score 25 or higher, it means that you connect to that archetype best and that archetype story is easy to bring into your life.

- If you score 10 or less, it means that you are uncomfortable with that archetype within yourself or within others.

The Archetypes

PART A

RULER

(Claims own power for good or for ill)

PART B

SAGE

(Attains wisdom, seeks truth, handles ambiguity, matches methodology to the task at hand)

PART C

MAGICIAN

(Creates opportunities to make your dreams come true. combination of creator and destroyer)

PART D

JESTER

(Enjoys and speaks the truth)

[This quiz has been adapted from carolynmamchur.com]

11.
THE LONG-LASTING REWARD OF SHADOW WORK

Exploring our inner shadows helps us better grasp the tricky swings of our feelings and the ways we connect with ourselves and everything around us. It provides support in unearthing more self-softness and self-embrace. It does this by helping us pinpoint where our current challenges came from in our past, shined down as crucial life tools. True, this process can drain us and be tough. Yet, the advantages of exploring our inner shadows centers on obtaining a deeper self-knowing, which "creates a sturdy base for us to reshape thinking patterns and world connections that aren't helping us anymore.

Mental Well-Being

Understanding yourself better with shadow work can make you more gentle to yourself and the people you hold dear. It helps lessen blame when dealing with others, and trims down bad or unhealthy fights. Our shadow self shows up when we feel unusually annoyed or grossed out by someone else's behavior. It's often a sign of a trait we have ignored within us. Spotting these sorts of hidden projections is key. With this practice, you'll likely develop more sympathy and understanding for others, especially those you've judged or disliked before. This method might also build your self-esteem and protection by looking deeply into qualities that annoy you about others. At the same time, it can cut down your feelings of shame and the pressure to be perfect.

Working on your shadow side might let you find, accept, and reconnect with aspects and dreams suppressed due to various reasons, and still affects who you are and your joy today. Suppose you were an inventive kid with dreams of becoming an artist, but you grew up in a household that didn't appreciate creative pursuits or claimed they weren't good career paths. You might have suppressed that part of yourself in your shadow.

You may have picked a respectable career, yet feel detached from your real passions, and shadow work might help. It helps you embrace and cherish hidden desires—reviving them in your awareness and merging your concealed self. It's mostly about a deep dive into past traits, choices, and actions that shaped your life—and what you didn't strive for or the individual you didn't turn into. This tool is awesome for living authentically. It assists us in taking off our seldom worn societal mask, and re finding what naturally fascinated and delighted us when we were kids.

Losing the inner dislike you might not realize you carry when you hide your darker side is possible. However, it's only doable by wholly acknowledging that part of yourself and continually practicing self-awareness.

Embracing your shadow means acknowledging every part of you with self-compassion. This may not always be easy or automatic. Yet starting shadow work opens the possibility for you to reach this state.

You can apply shadow work to discover your hidden gems—mostly, your unknown abilities and supplies that before you were completely unaware of.

Some folks might worry that their darkness might be too big to conquer. Usually, this dazzling brightness covers a lot of room. It just never got a chance to flourish previously.

Hiding your inner struggles can cause many issues. These problems might not be clear until you're prepared to confront these struggles. Working with your shadow can guide you to gain power over your health path, starting from the foundation. Not just handling certain health topics, such as stress or bad bonds, shadow work deals with the core reasons.

Shadow work also deals with exploring our unconscious mind. It helps find emotions we've pushed away, beliefs we've hidden, and parts of ourselves we've silenced. By facing these shadows, people learn more about the hidden patterns in their subconscious. These patterns impact our feelings, thoughts, and actions.

Shadow work means recognizing and accepting the parts of yourself that aren't as attractive. Realizing this leads to a better understanding of yourself, enabling people to welcome their complete self by joining the sunny and dark sides together. It also helps people identify signals—situations that bring out powerful feelings. By knowing these signals, people learn about unsettled problems, untreated injuries, or hidden feelings. This helps them better understand what's inside them. By tackling tricky feelings through shadow work, people learn more about their emotions. This deep dive helps them understand their emotions better, leading to the ability to handle emotions in a healthier way.

Shadow work can often reveal how our hidden selves affect how we interact with others. By knowing our shadows, we can see how they might shape our talks, actions, and friendships. This can bring more honest and kind-hearted connections. It also gives people the push they need to accept once ignored parts of themselves. Combining these elements and saying yes to self-love propels individual development. It ends in a truly honest, tough, and self-conscious lifestyle.

Remember that working on your inner self sets the stage for solid and lasting personal improvement over time. This comes from deep thinking, knowing oneself, and wholesome growth. Doing shadow work starts your deep dive into self-understanding and unity. You face buried emotions, accept shadow parts, and discover hidden routines. People begin an inside healing process. This healing trip helps people face old hurts, shocks, or restricting ideas. This clears the path for handling feelings better and finding inner calm.

Also, dealing with hidden issues helps us better understand our whole self. By looking at and accepting our hidden self, we feel more complete. This helps us accept who we are and treat ourselves with kindness. We don't judge or feel bad about our complex sides. Understanding ourselves lays the foundation for true growth and change.

Additionally, shadow work accelerates self-growth. It leads to more self-knowledge by investigating the shadow parts. It helps people learn more about their drives, actions, and relationships, which in turn inspires more conscious decisions in line with their core beliefs and goals. This boosted understanding enables folks to handle life's struggles with increased tenacity, flexibility and insight.

Plus, combining unseen traits boosts emotional smarts and cultivates better bonds. When folks grasp and fuse formerly unseen feelings and habits, they tune in more to their emotions and other people's emotions. This higher emotional savvy brings about more compassionate relationships and better face to face dynamics, nurturing richer, stronger connections.

In the end, shadow work has a lasting effect on self-development. It promotes an ongoing process of figuring oneself out, getting better, and changing. When people bring their hidden parts into their aware self, they set up the base for steady betterment, toughness, and a truly rewarding lifestyle.

Embracing The Lifelong Journey

How soon you'll see the outcomes of shadow work differs for each individual. You should do shadow work with calmness and realize that its benefits may not show up right away. Certain people might spot small changes in their mindset, feelings control, or friendships pretty soon, within weeks or months of steady use. These transformations might show as a deeper understanding of themselves, better emotional strength, or genuine chats with others.

However, in more profound, deep rooted changes or tackling complicated matters, things might need more time—sometimes stretching over months or even years. Revealing and assimilating deeply ingrained thoughts, unsettled events, or hidden sections usually calls for steady effort, self-observation, and readiness to face unease.

Moreover, different things can change how quickly shadow work moves along. These can be how serious the issues are, how dedicated the person is, the type of help they have, and the methods they use.

In shadow work, the timetable for seeing outcomes is different for everyone. You might find hints that you're moving forward. Such hints could be understanding yourself better, dealing more effectively with tough feelings, better talking in your relationships, or feeling calm and okay with yourself.

Sticking to a routine and dedication play crucial roles in how quickly and deeply you see results. Regular involvement in reflection activities like meditating, writing in a journal, or attending therapy sessions focusing on shadow work can speed things up. These activities provide a steady platform for self-examination. This allows a person to delve deeper into their hidden thoughts and blend their shadow elements more efficiently.

Furthermore, applauding tiny wins and recognizing minor changes in thinking, acting, or emotional reactions can mean progress. For example, seeing a kinder approach to yourself or others, sensing more stability in tough circumstances, or spotting a reduction in impulsive actions may display the slow blending of shadow elements.

Sure, it's crucial to be practical when dealing with shadow work. Don't expect instant solutions. Instead, see it as a deep, steady journey. Some hidden parts might need more time to find or blend, calling for dedication and patience.

One must value the journey in its entirety and not just the immediate outcomes. The fruits of personal reflection may not be instant, but they are profound. This process fuels personal development and understanding. Believing in the process, remaining dedicated to self-discovery, and exercising self-kindness on the journey may result in a more rewarding and impactful experience.

Keep in mind, the path of inner exploration matters as much as the end goal. Accept the exploration itself as a personal development part. Every move, no matter the speed, adds to self-knowledge. It strengthens resilience, genuine nature, and peace from within over time.

Finding Your Shadow Work Community

Finding a friendly group for shadow work can significantly boost your self-discovery and development journey. Check out these steps for help in finding and establishing a shadow work community:

INTERNET CHATS AND COMMUNITIES

Visit web based spaces, chats, or social media circles focused on shadow work. Places like Reddit, Facebook circles, or traditional forums regularly provide arenas for swapping stories, ideas, and tools related to shadow work. Participating in these groups opens up relationships with people who share your interests and are on the same journey.

EDUCATION EVENTS

Go to short courses, meetings, or secluded get togethers for shadow work. These are unique chances to meet others who are also into self-discovery. Joining shared tasks, talks, or planned sessions helps to build togetherness and shared learning moments.

GROUPS OF FUNCTIONS

Look for groups nearby or functions discussing psychology, personal betterment, or self-growth. Usually, these meetings have chats or practical sessions on shadow work. Making connections with folk in your neighborhood can end up in creating helpful friendships and growing a group sharing common interests.

HELP SESSIONS

Think about joining group help meetings or programs that focus on shadow work. These sessions are designed and offer a planned, comforting space to review the shadow aspects with others who have the same difficulties. These spots give instructions from skilled experts and a safe space for talking about experiences.

BUILD YOUR OWN GROUP

When a ready to go shadow work group isn't around, think about starting your own. Kick off a chat group, reading circle, or consistent meet to discuss shadow work in your neighborhood. Many websites can assist in bringing together folks eager to embark on this journey as a team.

INTERNET CLASSES AND SEMINARS

Join internet classes or seminars focused on shadow work. There are heaps of web platforms that present classes led by authorities in psychology and self-improvement. Getting involved in these classes can connect you with a group of folks chasing the same route of growth.

Creating or forming a group focused on shadow work is centered on forming a place for equal support, group learning, and motivation toward self-understanding. It doesn't matter if it's a virtual or physical meet up, being with others involved in shadow work can grant priceless knowledge, acknowledgment, and a feeling of unity.

Expanding Your Shadow Work Knowledge

To learn more about shadow work, plunge into a wealth of sources and routines. This will enhance both your grasp and use of this life changing procedure.

BOOKS ON SHADOW WORK

Dive into numerous books about shadow work authored by experts such as psychologists, therapists, and spiritual guide. Carl Jung, Debbie Ford, Robert A. Johnson, and more have provided deep understanding about the theory and practice of shadow work. Search for books that match your curiosity and method of self-exploration.

CLASSES AND LEARNING SESSIONS

Sign up for classes, workshops, or online programs focused on shadow work. There are several platforms with courses conducted by skilled experts. They give detailed direction, tasks, and methods to go deeper into shadow work practices.

EXPERT HELP
Think about getting help from therapists, counselors, or shadow work coaches. Their individual help or group therapy suggestions can offer special support. This can give deeper understanding and unique ways to handle certain problems.

THOUGHT LOGS AND SELF-THINKING
Make a habit of regular log creation as a self-thinking exercise. Inscribe your experiences, feelings, aspirations, and learnings from personal examination sessions for much needed introspection and self-learning. Self-thinking routines assist in understanding and transferring the newly obtained wisdom into everyday life.

FINDING CALM
Include calmness practices like focusing and quiet time in your every day. Focusing helps you pay attention to feelings and thoughts, so you can learn about hidden patterns. Quiet times give mental sharpness and a good space for studying the unknown parts of you.

ARTISTIC EXPLORATION
Use art, music, dance, or stories to investigate and display hidden parts. Artistic activities enable silent study and can reveal more about our subconscious mind.

TALK AND LEARN TOGETHER
Connect with others doing shadow work. Use internet forums, group chats, or go to gatherings to swap ideas. You can learn from different viewpoints and get help from those on similar paths.

NEVER ENDING DISCOVERY
Adopt a spirit of endless learning and discovery. Stay receptive to fresh thoughts, concepts, and methods in shadow work. Participate in talks, workshops, or symposiums on psychology, spirituality, or self-improvement to broaden your understanding.

Learning about shadow work needs a layered strategy combining theory, practice, and personal events. Use various resources and methods to boost your understanding and promote change during your shadow work exploration.

ACTIVITY 10: The Mirror

Follow the steps below to enquire about your shadow self:

1. Peaceful Pondering: Pick a quiet, calm spot and sit easy. Draw in several big breaths to center your thoughts and focus on the here and now.

2. Looking at Reflections: Think about a figurative mirror before you. It shows your hidden self—the parts you're aware of, portrayed by your ego, and the unseen parts, signified by your shadow.

3. Self-Reflection: Start by gazing at your reflection in the mirror. Ponder on the parts of yourself that feel like "you." These could be your ideas, convictions, or characteristics. Consider how these parts have molded your self-image and steered your life decisions.

4. Shadow Discovery: Now, turn your attention to the hidden parts of you the silent shadows in the mirror's reach. These might include unaddressed feelings, suppressed wishes, or features you generally disregard. Understand these parts too add to your completeness, despite them possibly conflicting with how you see yourself.

5. Understanding the Dark: Have a kind chat with the shadows. Consider asking things like "What do you want to tell me?" or "How have you unknowingly impacted my actions?" Let their responses emerge without any judgment or fright.

6. Joining and Recovery: Welcome the dark places with knowledge and affection. Know that they're vital elements of your mind and can provide useful understandings. Don't push them away or ignore them; rather, try to absorb their helpful advice into your active mind.

7. Self Improvement Pledge: Create a hopeful pledge that highlights your dedication to accept and combine your dark sides into your self-concept. Here's an instance, "I recognize and welcome every part of me, and through self-consciousness, I encounter expansion and completeness."

8. Keep Discovering Yourself: When you finish up the activity, bear in mind that this self-reflection journey isn't over. Maintain routine checks of self-understanding to enhance recognition and encourage individual progress.

CONCLUSION

Shadow work is a deep journey of self-learning and unity. It goes far beyond just looking at our hidden sides. It's a powerful expedition into the heart of human feelings. Diving into the shadows helps us to accept the many parts of us, face hidden feelings, and understand the multi sided nature of our lives. Carl Jung's idea explains this process. It shows the shadow doesn't only contain our dark sides but also the opportunity for our growth and completeness.

The hurdles we face in shadow work—like pushback, emotional chaos, to feeling exposed and handling scares—highlight its depth and importance. But it's within these hurdles that shadow work's secret changes come to light. With patience, understanding, and grit, we navigate these obstacles, aiming for healing, development, and wholeness.

Shadow work and inner child healing connect past actions to current feelings. This offers a road to mend old, deep hurts. Doing shadow work can help you look inside yourself. Methods like thinking deeply, picturing things, and understanding dreams help explore hidden feelings. This leads to being more self-aware and understanding your emotions better.

The path of self-discovery is ongoing, slowly building resilience, truth, and deep self-understanding. Walking this path means finding or building a helping group, always learning more, and realizing the change that patience and self-love can create.

Shadow work isn't some abstract idea; it's an impactful philosophical voyage—a path directing us to accept our whole being. It's a continuing task that brings us nearer to knowing, agreeing with, and combining all aspects of our essence—the bright, the back, and the in between. On this mission, we don't just discover secrets within us but create an opportunity for major personal progress, recovery, and an authentic lifestyle.

Shadow work is a slow and steady endeavor. No need for hurry or pressure. Grasp the nuances of your inner self, and see that knowing you is an exciting journey. Engage with your faults, as they help unlock your true identity. Keep in mind that you're capable, hardy, and deserving of a life enriched with self-realization and affection. You've got this!

www.ingramcontent.com/pod-product-compliance
Lightning Source LLC
Chambersburg PA
CBHW080523030426
42337CB00023B/4611